NATIONAL GEOGRAPHIC KiDS

PET RECORDS

JULIE BEER AND MICHELLE HARRIS

THE WEIRDEST, CUTEST, BIGGEST, COOLEST, TINIEST, AND SMARTEST PETS ON THE PLANET

NATIONAL GEOGRAPHIC
WASHINGTON, D.C.

CHAPTER 5: **CUTEST** 122

CHAPTER 6: **MOST ATHLETIC** 148

CHAPTER 7: **MOST POPULAR** 176

PETS OFFER ANTICS, LAUGHS, AND LOTS AND LOTS OF LOVE.

They can range from cuddly cats to leaping lizards, from *fin*-tastic fish to bold birds, from lovable pups to slithering snakes. In National Geographic Kids *Pet Records*, you'll meet record-breaking dogs and cats as well as prizewinning pigs and parakeets. You'll discover fascinating facts about pets you see every day and some you've maybe never seen before, pets that camp out in tiny apartments and some that make their homes on sprawling farms.

Before you dive into the winners, a few reminders: *Pet Records* is a book with our picks for the raddest record-breaking pets on the planet. It's also a book with animal besties, furry friends that come to the aid of their humans, and pets that help scientists solve modern problems. While each chapter crowns a champion and awards runners-up, there is more than one way to ponder a pet. So, no matter where we pin the award, go ahead and choose your own champions.

What are you waiting for? There are superstars on every page!

Be a Kind Companion

We owe it to our soft and scaly friends to give them the space and care they need to thrive. Animals should never be taken from the wild, so be sure to research where your potential pet came from. Some species are illegally caught and then sold or bred in crowded and unsafe conditions. If you are considering getting an "exotic" pet like a python or hedgehog, have an adult check local laws (not all pets are welcome in all places). And always buy from a responsible seller, or, better yet, consider giving a rescue pet their forever home.

Throughout the book, you'll see this red paw-print icon next to some pets. The icon tells you that this kind of animal may be particularly vulnerable to harmful practices in the exotic pet trade. Although every new pet calls for thought and planning, these pets may require extra research and care and should always be adopted rather than bought.

CHAPTER 1

GET READY TO MEET THE MOST MASSIVE PETS IN THE WORLD.

These pets may all be big winners, but not all of them boast a big body. Some are the tallest, longest, or heaviest for their groups, while others take home the prize for more surprising reasons.

BIGGEST 11

THE GREAT DANE

First bred in Germany to hunt wild boar, the regal Great Dane is paws down a true giant among pets. This massive working dog can stand taller than 30 inches (76 cm) at the shoulder—and when it rears up on its hind legs, it's taller than most people! This friendly but steadfast guardian is also no lightweight: A fully grown male Great Dane can weigh as much as a fully grown adult human.

IN GERMANY, THE BREED IS KNOWN AS **DEUTSCHE DOGGE.**

THE GREAT DANE IS PENNSYLVANIA'S **STATE DOG.**

NICKNAME: **THE APOLLO OF DOGS**

HEIGHT, FEMALE: **AT LEAST 28 INCHES (71 CM) AT SHOULDER**

HEIGHT, MALE: **AT LEAST 30 INCHES (76 CM) AT SHOULDER**

WEIGHT, FEMALE: **UP TO 140 POUNDS (63 KG)**

WEIGHT, MALE: **UP TO 175 POUNDS (79 KG)**

LIFE SPAN: **10 YEARS**

RECORD HOLDER: **44 INCHES (1.2 M) AT SHOULDER**

BIGGEST·13

Find out how these other gargantuan greats tip the scales to come out on top.

BIGGEST BIRD

HYACINTH MACAW

Hyacinth macaws are the giants of the bird world. The largest type of parrot, these tropical birds from parts of Brazil and Paraguay can reach lengths of 40 inches (101 cm), weigh about 3.5 pounds (1.6 kg), and have a wingspan stretching five feet (1.5 m) wide! Hyacinth macaws achieve their avian heft through a steady diet of flowers, seeds, and nectar. Thanks to its brilliant blue feathers and the yellow ring around its eyes, there is no missing this magnificent macaw.

BIGGEST **HOUSE CAT**
MAINE COON

This furry record holder is the state cat of Maine, U.S.A.—go figure! And it's definitely not an itty-bitty kitty. Male Maine coons can weigh 25 pounds (11 kg) or more, with females weighing just a few pounds less, and when kittens, these cats can grow twice as fast as other kittens. It's also one of the oldest long-haired breeds in the United States. The Maine coon's long hair, tufted paws, and fluffy tail help keep this *purr*-fect pet warm during harsh northern winters.

BIGGEST **LIZARD**
GREEN IGUANA

The green iguana wins this category tails down. These green goliaths can be more than six feet (1.8 m) long and weigh about 11 pounds (5 kg). But green iguanas don't get that big by being ravenous meat eaters; instead, these herbivores gain their girth by chowing down on flowers, fruits, and veggies. They require a lot of specialized care, so do your research before making this beasty your bestie.

BIGGEST **RABBIT**
DARIUS

Think bunnies are cute little fluff balls hopping along the hedgerows? Not this guy! Darius, a Flemish giant rabbit, is four feet three inches (129.5 cm) long. That's longer than most second graders are tall! These intelligent rabbits stand on their hind legs to better see the world around them. And they even play fetch with their owners, just like dogs.

MORE RUNNERS-UP ...

Grab a ringside seat and settle in for more heavyweight honorable mentions.

BIGGEST RODENT

CAPYBARA

These South American rodents are the world's biggest, and 60 times heavier than their regular-size relatives, such as rock cavies and guinea pigs! Capybaras stand two feet (0.6 m) tall and can be four feet (1.2 m) long—about the same as a medium-size dog. They're also no lightweights, tipping the scales at more than 150 pounds (68 kg). Capybaras are great swimmers, able to hold their breath underwater for minutes at a time. In the wild, capybaras live in groups; they are extremely social animals, so experts recommend that, when kept as pets, they should also have buddies.

BIGGEST INSECT

WALKING STICK

A giant insect that can turn into a superskinny stick? That might sound like the plot of a science-fiction movie, but these beauties are most certainly real. Stick insects can grow to be longer than 12 inches (30 cm), and while you might think it would be easy to spot such big critters, walking sticks are camouflage pros, blending in with the twigs and branches where they live. These easy-to-keep pets can be escape artists, though, so make sure they "stick" close to home.

BIGGEST **DONKEY**
ROMULUS

If you think of donkeys as small and stubborn, this gargantuan winner will change your mind. Romulus, an American Mammoth Jackstock, measures five feet eight inches (173 cm) tall—that's as tall as a grown man!—and weighs 1,200 pounds (544 kg). None other than U.S. president George Washington helped introduce this hefty breed—prized for its ability to pull heavy loads—to the United States as the perfect helper to have on the farm.

BIGGEST **TORTOISE**
GIANT TORTOISE

The largest giant tortoises can weigh a whopping 500 pounds (225 kg)—as much as a tiger! And their shells measure an amazing five feet (1.5 m) across. These gentle giants have giant life spans to match and, when kept as pets, can easily outlive their owners. A giant tortoise named Jonathan was given to the governor of St. Helena (a remote island in the South Atlantic) in the late 1800s. He was gussied up for a visit from the British royal family in 2016—when Jonathan was 184 years old!

OVER-GROWN

For some animals, size is limitless!

GREEN TREE PYTHON

When you adopt a new kitten, you can make a pretty good guess about how big she's going to be when she grows up: maybe 8 to 12 pounds (3.6 to 5.4 kg), depending on the breed. In fact, it's relatively easy to get a ballpark estimate of how big most mammals will grow to be—including humans! Yes, family genetics and nutrition can vary peoples' sizes quite a bit, but in general, our skeletons reach a certain size and stop growing once we reach adulthood.

That's not the case with most fish, amphibians, and reptiles, which are known as indeterminate growers. Imagine this: After you're born, you grow quite quickly (like all kids do), but once you become an adult, instead of leveling out, you just keep slowly growing. That growth chart on the wall where your parents pencil in your height each year just keeps getting higher and higher—your entire life! That would be a pretty cool superpower.

But wait ... if some animals grow forever, why don't we see enormous lizards or turtles crawling around? Two reasons: Growing continues, but it is a slow growth. Also, nature has a checks-and-balances system: The longer an animal lives, the more likely it will come into contact with predators and diseases. Unlike the animals we keep as pets, animals in the wild often don't live as long, so they don't have time to grow as big.

TRUE OR FALSE: SNAKES AND LIZARDS GROW ONLY AS BIG AS THEIR HABITAT WILL ALLOW. *False! No matter the size of their enclosure, they will continue to slowly grow. So it's important to make sure you provide a space that continues to be big enough throughout their lives.*

HERMIT CRABS: TIME FOR AN UPGRADE

We've all been there: Our favorite shirt that we wear all the time suddenly starts to feel a bit ... snug. The sleeves are too tight, and it's a wee bit too short to tuck in. Ugh! Growth spurt! This is exactly what hermit crabs go through ... their whole life. Hermit crabs are an example of an animal that never stops growing—so every so often they need to change their outfit (aka their shell). In the wild, hermit crabs go looking for an abandoned shell, usually left by a snail. When hermit crabs are kept as pets, their keepers need to provide the larger shells for them. (It's key to have different sizes available so they can find just the right fit.) Hermit crabs need the shells to protect their soft abdomen, and the perfect shell is the one with the right-size hole they can squeeze into. Once they get too big for it, they are once again on the hunt for an upgrade!

BIGGEST APPETITES

Whether they snack all day or chow down on one mega-meal, these pets have all eaten their way into the record book.

VEGGIE-LOVING **SWINE**

VIETNAMESE POTBELLIED PIGS

Think these porkers have big appetites? While they do love to eat—and can weigh more than 100 pounds (45 kg)—Vietnamese potbellied pigs are health fanatics of a sort: Veggies make up about a quarter of their diets. And these pets are smart enough to figure out how to get into the fridge, so be sure to keep an eye on the lettuce!

HUNGRY, HUNGRY **CANINE**

OLD ENGLISH MASTIFF

All puppies need to eat a lot of food as they grow, but Old English mastiff puppies really take the cake—or in this case, the chow. Six-month-old puppies can eat 12 cups (1,800 g) of food a day, which makes sense, since a full-grown mastiff can weigh as much as a National Football League quarterback!

HEFTY **HORSE**

SHIRES

The shire is a draft horse used to carrying heavy loads. After all, its ancestors carried knights wearing as much as 400 pounds (181 kg) of armor into battle! Today, these hefty horses can weigh more than 2,000 pounds (907 kg), with appetites to match. These mighty munchers can eat 50 pounds (23 kg) of grain and hay a day.

BINGE-EATING **REPTILE**

BURMESE PYTHON

These cold-blooded snakes like to space out their warm-blooded snacks; they may go months between meals. But when it's time to chow down once again, what a meal it is! Weighing more than 250 pounds (110 kg), Burmese pythons can eat up to a quarter of their body weight in one sitting, meaning they could be gearing up for a 60-pound (27-kg) dinner!

THOUSANDS OF KITTIES BECKON IN JAPAN.

Here's a place that's sure to put a cat-like grin on your face: Visitors to Gotokuji Temple in Tokyo, Japan, are greeted with waves by an army of "beckoning cats"—statues that are mostly white with a red collar, red ears, and a raised paw. But there's more to these cordial kitties than a friendly hello.

According to local legend, centuries ago there was a poor monk who was taking care of a temple and struggling to make ends meet, but he always shared his food with his beloved cat. One day the monk asked the cat to bring him good fortune. Soon after, a wealthy, powerful lord came across the cat, which waved him into the monk's temple. Without warning, a thunderstorm struck. But the lord was already safe inside. Impressed that the cat had helped him escape the storm, the lord made a donation to improve the temple. Today, that temple is Gotokuji, and the *maneki-neko*, or beckoning cat, statues have become a symbol of good fortune in Japan and across Asia. Gotokuji has more beckoning cats than any other temple, with thousands of big and small statues lined up, waving at visitors. And the population continues to grow: Various sizes of the statues can be purchased on-site and then, after a wish or prayer for good luck is made, they are left at the temple.

RIGHTY OR LEFTY: WHAT'S THE DIFFERENCE?

Waving cat, beckoning cat, good-luck cat ... there are lots of different names for these feline statues and—depending on the paw they're waving—different meanings, too. At Gotokuji Temple, most of the statues have a right paw raised. That generally means protection at home, which relates to the story of the cat and the lord. A left-paw-waving cat invites success in business. You might find one of these statues in a store or restaurant.

KOI CAN GET **SUNBURNED!** WHEN KEPT IN OUTDOOR PONDS, THEY NEED **PLENTY** OF **SHADE.**

COLOSSAL KOI

Calling this substantial swimmer "Big Girl" is an understatement! At 90 pounds (41 kg), Big Girl is triple the size of a typical koi and even outweighs the average 11-year-old kid! The world's largest koi, Big Girl is also a whopping four feet long (1.2 m). Big Girl was born in Japan, but a British koi collector bought her and brought her home to England.

Although they may look like oversize goldfish, koi and goldfish are not the same species; they do, however, share carp as their common ancestor. A major difference between koi and goldfish is that koi don't swim in bowls! They need a pond with plenty of room to swish their fins. While they can live in aquariums, most are kept outdoors in ponds or water gardens.

Modern Japanese koi date to the 19th century, where they were kept by rice farmers and eventually bred for their colorful spots. A koi's average life span is 40 years, but some have lived much longer. A record-setting example? A koi named Hanako, which was said to have lived to be 226! Researchers determined Hanako's age by counting the rings in her fish scales, much like how rings in a tree's trunk approximate the age of the tree.

BATTLE OF THE BIGGEST

Who will prevail in these massive matchups?

BIGGEST NOISEMAKER

Sorry, pups, but birds win in this sound-off. The loudest dog bark ever measured was 113.1 decibels by a golden retriever. But a Moluccan cockatoo can squawk as loud as 129 decibels—that's louder than a chain saw!

WINNER

COCKATOO **vs.** DOG

WINNER

BIGGEST PET CELEBRITY

The cute factor of these two pups has gone seriously viral. But in terms of social media popularity, Jiffpom the Pomeranian beats out Doug the Pug by several million devoted fans.

JIFFPOM **vs.** DOUG THE PUG

WINNER

ENGLISH LOP RABBIT vs. BLOODHOUND

BIGGEST EARS

The bunnies leaped ahead in this battle. While a bloodhound named Tigger had ears that measured more than 13 inches (33 cm) in length, the ears on an English lop named Nipper's Geronimo had a complete span of 31 inches (79 cm).

BIGGEST TRUFFLE HUNTER

Lagotti Romagnoli may look like teddy bears, but these curly-haired Italian dogs have a nose for truffles—the pricey fungus delicacy that grows near tree roots. They are happy to sniff them out and turn them over to claim a treat reward from their human. Pigs, on the other hand, who were traditionally used to find truffles, often gobbled them up before people could collect them!

WINNER

DOG vs. PIG

AFGHAN HOUND vs. PERUVIAN GUINEA PIG

TIE

BIGGEST HAIRDO

Both Afghan hounds and Peruvian guinea pigs are equally known for their long, silky hair. And they require lots of maintenance to keep it tangle-free. This smack-down isn't worth getting ourselves knotted up over. Let's call it a tie!

THE GREAT DANE
WEIGH-IN!

1
GREAT =
DANE

3
EIGHT-YEAR-
OLD KIDS

50
HYACINTH
MACAWS

29
CHIHUAHUAS

536 iPHONES

1 LARGE AARDVARK

2 CHEETAHS

700 QUARTER-POUND HAMBURGERS

THE LARGEST SNAKE THAT EVER SLITHERED

TITANOBOA CERREJONENSIS

TIME PERIOD: **66 TO 56 MILLION YEARS AGO**

LOCATION: **NORTHEASTERN COLOMBIA, SOUTH AMERICA**

LENGTH: **48 FEET (14.6 M)**

WEIGHT: **1.25 TONS (1.1 T)**

Around 66 million years ago—a few million years after most dinosaurs became extinct—a new fearsome predator slithered onto the South American continent: *Titanoboa cerrejonensis,* a snake as long as a bus and as heavy as a rhino.

Titanoboa looked a bit like a modern boa constrictor, but it behaved like a modern anaconda, meaning it could swim in fast-moving rivers and also slink through swamps. To maintain its outsize proportions, it had to eat ... a lot—likely fish, turtles, and even crocodiles. Its head alone was two feet long (0.6 m), and its jaw could open nearly 180 degrees. That's big enough to swallow a motorcycle!

In the world of superheroes, it would take a chemical experiment gone very bad to make such a remarkably massive reptile. Not the case with *Titanoboa,* whose super size was likely climate related. Reptiles grow bigger in warm climates, and we know from fossil discoveries that *Titanoboa* lived in South America (where both boa constrictors and anacondas are common today), which was warmer than it is now. Some researchers say that intense tropical heat is what allowed *Titanoboa* to grow to become the largest snake that ever slithered on Earth.

TITANOBOA IS AN ANCESTOR OF TODAY'S **BOAS** AND **ANACONDAS.**

BIGGEST 31

BIG-AT-A-GLANCE

BLOODHOUND

CHAMELEON

GECKO

1 BIGGEST SNIFFER

Smell a winner? It's got to be a bloodhound. Bloodhounds can distinguish smells 1,000 times better than you can! They have 40 times more "scent receptors" than humans do and an instinctual drive to follow their nose. Some have stuck to a trail for more than 130 miles (209 km), meaning that when following a specific scent, a bloodhound will pursue it until the source is found or the scent disappears.

2 BIGGEST CHATTERBOX

Think reptiles are the silent type? Not geckos! They're known for their chirps and barks. This chattering is a form of communication—it either lets other geckos know to back off their territory or is a way to attract a mate. Don't understand gecko? You're not alone. Some of their sounds aren't even audible to humans!

4 BIGGEST TONGUE

Chameleons are champion slurpers: Their tongues stretch more than twice their body length! In adult humans that would equal a tongue the length of 10 to 12 feet (about 3 to 4 m). Relative to chameleons' size, their tongue is longer than any other vertebrate's.

NEWFOUNDLAND

STICKY SNEAKY ATTACK

A chameleon's tongue can accelerate from zero to 60 miles an hour (97 km/h) in 1/100th of a second—twice as fast as the fastest race car! How does it do it? The chameleon's tongue is made of elastic tissue that folds up like an accordion, and when it's released, it's like an arrow being shot out from a bow. Bugs never even know what nabbed them!

5 BIGGEST EYES

A horse's eyes may not appear all that enormous relative to its large head, but they are record-holding big—the biggest of any land mammal! The placement of those peepers is an advantage: Because they're on the sides of the head, rather than in front (like humans' eyes), horses have almost 360-degree vision. They do, however, have two blind spots: directly in front of them and directly behind them!

6 BIGGEST PAWS

Big feet? More like big flippers! Newfoundlands' paws are wide and webbed. That lets them do what they like best: swim! Those strong, powerful paws allow them to paddle efficiently through water. The pads on their feet are also extra thick, adapted for walking around in colder climates.

8 BIGGEST TEETH

How long are the longest teeth if they never stop growing? Infinitely long! A rabbit's teeth grow continuously throughout its life. That may sound a little awkward, especially when it comes to eating, but luckily they're also constantly worn down by chewing! Rabbits grind their teeth together when they chew, so there's no maintenance required.

HORSE

RABBIT

TORTOISE SHELLS GIVE DESIGNERS BIG IDEAS.

TORTOISES DON'T HAVE TEETH.

Imagine having to carry your house around with you—all the time! Our pet tortoises do just that.

Tortoises and turtles are the only reptiles that have a bony shell. The shell is made up of honeycomb-shaped structures that surround small air chambers. This makes it strong enough to protect the reptile's large body underneath yet lightweight enough not to be a burden. And since they've been around for some 200 million years, nature worked out elements of architectural design, such as buttresses and arches, in their shells long before humans used those same ideas to build cathedrals and bridges.

Tortoises' shells are not only superstrong and relatively lightweight, but they also protect their bodies from the sun and help regulate their body temperature, which is a good thing for tortoises that live in hot environments. And that function gave two researchers at Alexandria University in Egypt a smart idea. They studied the shell of the Egyptian tortoise, a small desert-dwelling tortoise from northern Africa, and found that the solar radiation falling on the tortoise shell was less than that falling on a standard architectural dome. In computer models that made structural changes to the shape of a dome based on the dimensions of the Egyptian tortoise's shell, there was a reduction in the heat load under a standard dome of more than 10 percent. That would keep people cooler as well as save energy. Brilliant!

BIG **BIGGER** BEST!

Can you tell the difference between big and humongous? Rank these critters in order from smallest to biggest, then check out our answer key, below, to see how you did!

BIG GIRL KOI FISH

GREEN IGUANA

36

HYACINTH MACAW

MAINE COON CAT

GREAT DANE

WALKING STICK

TITANOBOA

CHAPTER 2

GOOD THINGS REALLY DO COME IN SMALL PACKAGES.

The pets in this chapter may be small in stature, but they are big in personality. Turn the page to meet some of the world's most compact companions.

THE SEA MONKEY
[BRINE SHRIMP]

They aren't monkeys, and they don't live in the sea, but sea monkeys can make fantastic first pets. First sold in the 1960s, they were known as instant pets. Why? Sea monkeys come in a dry packet and look like tiny specs of dust—as small as the dot of the letter *i*. These "monkeys" are really brine shrimp in a state of suspended animation. This state, known as cryptobiosis, allows the shrimp to survive until conditions for their growth improve. In the case of sea monkeys, this change happens when the "dust" is put into specially treated water, causing these aquatic animals to spring to life. While they start off small, in just a few weeks they can grow to be more than half an inch long (1.3 cm).

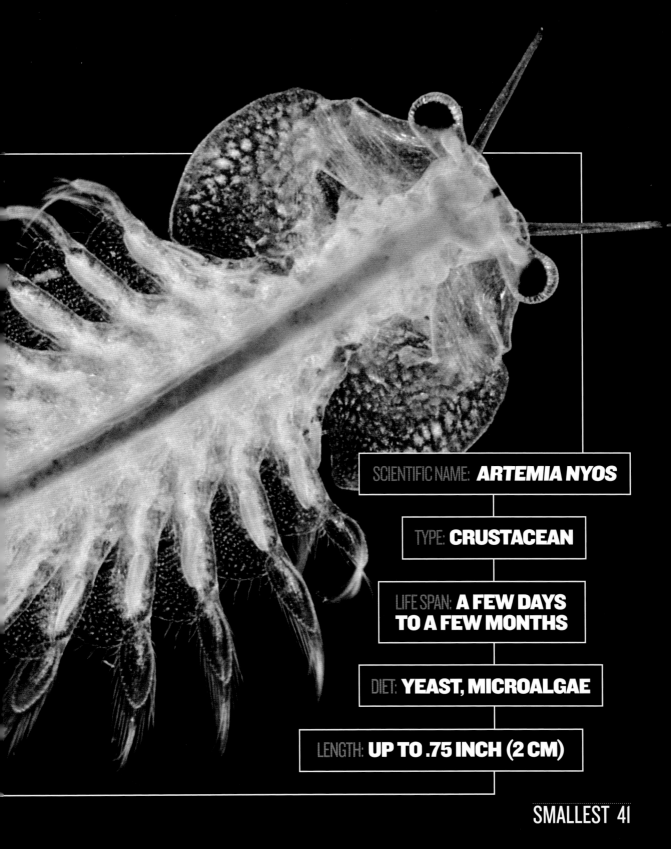

SCIENTIFIC NAME: **ARTEMIA NYOS**

TYPE: **CRUSTACEAN**

LIFE SPAN: **A FEW DAYS TO A FEW MONTHS**

DIET: **YEAST, MICROALGAE**

LENGTH: **UP TO .75 INCH (2 CM)**

THE RUNNERS-UP ...

These mighty minis are the smallest of their kind.

SMALLEST
PET LIZARD

GREEN ANOLE

Green anoles—the only lizard native to North America—grow to be only about six inches (15 cm) long. Males of this wee reptile species use a fanlike piece of skin on their throats to show off to females or when facing rivals. Special toe pads give them superb climbing abilities, as they scale walls and trees with ease. And when kept as pets, these small lizards can even be fed by hand.

SMALLEST PET AQUATIC FROG

AFRICAN DWARF FROG

This small swimmer grows to be only about three inches (7.5 cm) long. African dwarf frogs spend their lives submerged in water, coming to the surface to breathe, and are happiest with a few friends in their tank.

SMALLEST DOG

CHIHUAHUA

Weighing only about six pounds (3 kg), Chihuahuas have outsize personalities for their small size. They hold their ground against anyone, large or small, and are famous for being social media darlings as well as for being pampered by celebrities. Tough life!

SMALLEST CAT

SINGAPURA

These compact cats tip the scales at a mere five pounds (2.3 kg)—a fifth of what a Maine coon cat (p. 15) can weigh. The small winners were first bred in the early 1970s, but in that short time they have made a big impression. Curious and friendly, these felines like to play and will even sit on their human's shoulders to get a better look around.

These small animals are big fun on the farm.

SMALLEST **HORSE**

THUMBELINA

All miniature horses are miniature, of course. But a chestnut mare named Thumbelina is so small that she calls a doghouse home! Thumbelina weighs less than 60 pounds (27 kg) and stands 17.5 inches (44.5 cm) at the withers (the highest part of a horse's back, at the base of the neck above its shoulders). She is much smaller than even the average miniature horse, a breed that stands no more than 34 inches (86 cm) at the withers.

SMALLEST **GOAT**

PYGMY GOAT

At less than two feet (0.6 m) tall, these inquisitive little goats are just the right size for Thumbelina's doghouse. About as big as medium-size dogs, pygmy goats don't bark, but they do like to belch—as much as 10 liters' (think soda bottles) worth of gas an hour!

44

SMALLEST **COW**
MINIATURE ZEBU

At their tallest, miniature zebus stand just over three feet (0.9 m), about the same height as a three-year-old kid. This hardy breed of small cow was first bred thousands of years ago in South Asia. Zebus are recognizable by the hump (it's small, of course) on their upper backs; the hump is just an enlarged muscle.

SMALLEST **CHICKEN**
MALAYSIAN SERAMA

This breed of chicken—the world's smallest—weighs only about one pound (500 g) and, at just eight inches (20 cm) tall, is about the size of a toaster. First bred in the 1970s in Malaysia, these friendly fowl enjoy being around their human friends.

THIS "LITTLE" PIGGY!

Potbellied pigs, bred from domestic Vietnamese pig breeds, sometimes go by the nickname "teacup pigs" or "micro pigs." And when they are newborns, they are indeed small enough to spill out of a teacup. Squeal!

But there's a catch to these cuddly cuties: There's no such thing as a pig that stays mini. Potbellied pigs are cup-size only when they are babies and eventually grow to be between 100 and 175 pounds (45 and 79 kg)—about the weight of a Old English mastiff (p.20)!

Although teacup pigs grow to be big, many people still keep them indoors as house pets. They stand about two feet (0.6 m) tall, can be potty trained just like a dog, and—despite being associated with phrases like "messy as a pigpen"—are actually quite clean! Pigs that live outdoors often lie in the mud to cool off, but indoors their favorite snuggly spot is a comfy pillow or dog bed. People have found pigs to be such great companions that some even serve as emotional support animals.

"I WON'T STAY THIS SMALL FOR LONG!"

WHEN PIGS ARE OUTDOORS, ROLLING IN MUD PROTECTS THEIR SKIN FROM GETTING SUNBURNED.

SMALLEST 47

POCKET PETS

These petite rodents are all tiny enough to fit in your hand— or your pocket!

DUPRASI GERBIL

Caring for these small gerbils, also known as "fat-tails" or "doops," won't give your muscles a workout. The heaviest ones weigh only as much as a stick of butter! Their small size and light color help the four-inch (10-cm)-long duprasi survive in the deserts of northern Africa, where they burrow into the sand to avoid predators.

CHINCHILLA

Originally from the Andes mountain range in South America, chinchillas have been kept as pets since the time of the ancient Inca. These pint-size rodents have silky, dense fur to keep them warm in cooler temperatures. All that softness doesn't make them heavy, though—the fluffy lightweights tip the scales at less than two pounds (0.9 kg).

ROBOROVSKI DWARF HAMSTER

At only about two inches (5 cm) in length, these sandy brown hamsters are the smallest breed of popular pet hamsters. The tiny tots weigh less than a bar of chocolate! While the "Robo" has a lot of energy, it's usually not a fan of being held.

MOUSE

Like many rodents, these curious and intelligent pets are nocturnal—meaning they like to party at night. At only about four inches (10 cm) long, domestic mice will eat veggies right from their human's hands if time is spent getting to know them. And they like to play with toy ladders and balls.

GUINEA PIG

In the United States, there are 13 recognized breeds of this small rodent from South America. And that means there is a lot of variety to this pet: They come in many different colors and hair types—wiry, curly, silky, and fuzzy—and the Abyssinian breed even sports a "mustache." Most guinea pigs weigh about two pounds (1 kg), but you'd need a really large pocket for the biggest members of the group, which can weigh almost as much as a gallon (3.8 L) of water.

SMALLEST ANIMAL RESCUE

Cats and water don't usually mix, but in Amsterdam, the Netherlands, they are the *purr*-fect combination. The Catboat, located on a canal in Amsterdam, is a floating adoption center for abandoned cats. Don't worry: There's no risk of a cat going overboard. The houseboat is fully fenced, and while the curious kitties like to keep an eye on the ducks floating in the canal, they can't get out for a closer look.

About 15 cats are permanent residents of the houseboat, but the other 35 or so kitties are available for adoption. Adoptions are taken seriously on the Catboat. There's an application process, along with a trial period to make sure that the cat and human are the right fit. But even if you aren't ready to take a kitty home, you can still come aboard the Catboat: About 4,500 people a year stop by to play, brush the cats' coats, and snuggle.

MEOW-SEUM

After scratching the ears of some real cats on the Catboat, why not make a side trip over to Amsterdam's Kattenkabinet, or Cat Cabinet, a museum devoted to the role of cats in arts and culture? The museum was founded in 1990 by a Dutchman who wanted to honor his beloved orange cat. The collection includes paintings, books, sculptures, and posters—all with a focus on kitties.

DWARF RABBITS

What's cuter than a bunny? A bunny that continues to look like a baby bunny even after it's fully grown! Netherland dwarf rabbits grow to be only about two pounds (0.9 kg). Besides their half-pint proportions, what gives these petite pets babyish looks are their stubby ears, which stand up high on their heads.

There's more to the definition of a dwarf rabbit than being a lightweight and having elflike ears. Dwarf rabbits have a gene passed on from their parents that causes dwarfism. There are fewer than a dozen breeds of dwarf rabbits, with the smallest being the Netherland. Besides small ears, they have a compact body and a round head.

But just because they're small doesn't mean they like small spaces. On the contrary, Netherland dwarf rabbits are known for being high-energy, so they need lots of space to stretch their little legs. And that small exterior also comes with a big attitude! They have a reputation for being stubborn, so it's best to handle them a lot when they are babies so they get used to people.

ALL RABBITS, EVEN THE **TINIEST** ONES, USE THEIR **BIG BACK FEET** TO STOMP TO GET ATTENTION, SHOW THAT THEY'RE **MAD**, OR ALERT OTHER RABBITS TO DANGER.

BATTLE OF THE

Who's the mightier mini?

SMALLEST

MUNCHKIN CAT vs. CORGI

WINNER

SHORTEST LEGS

Even the Queen of England's famous corgis couldn't win this battle! A corgi's legs may be stubby, but a munchkin cat's legs are extra squat, sometimes barely long enough to get its belly off the ground.

HERMIT CRAB vs. MUSK TURTLE

SMALLEST SHELL

Musk turtles can fit in the palm of your hand, but they can't beat out super shrimpy hermit crabs. Typical pet hermit crabs are just a couple of inches (5 cm) long, half the size of a musk turtle. But hermit crabs in the wild can be as big as a coconut!

WINNER

WINNER

MOST SMALL DOGS PER CAPITA

The largest country in South America loves small dogs! Brazilians have more small dogs per capita than any other country in the world. (Runners-up are Portugal and Mexico.) Saudi Arabia, on the other hand, has more large dogs. Seventy percent of all dogs in the country are big, weighing more than 50 pounds (23 kg).

BRAZIL VS. **SAUDI ARABIA**

TINIEST BABY

In this battle of pig versus hog, the hog wins. Baby guinea pigs are enormously cute—about the size of the palm of your hand when they are born. But itty-bitty hedgehogs—whose spines begin to poke out only a few hours after they're born—are even smaller. Hedgehogs are only the size of a doughnut hole when they're three weeks old!

GUINEA PIG VS. **HEDGEHOG**

WINNER

AFRICAN GRAY PARROT VS. **CORN SNAKE**

TIE

SMALLEST EGG

What do a corn snake and an African gray parrot have in common? They start out the same size! Corn snakes and African grays lay eggs that are about the size of a walnut.

DWARF HAMSTERS

Get the digits on these dainty daredevils.

LENGTH AT BIRTH
0.8 inch (2 CM) LONG

AVERAGE LIFE SPAN IN CAPTIVITY
2-4 years

LENGTH FULLY GROWN
2-4 inches (5–10 CM) LONG

MAX LENGTH OF ROBO'S HAIR
0.4 inch (10 MM) LONG

WEIGHT FULLY GROWN
.75-2 ounces (21–57 G)

AVERAGE BODY
TEMPERATURE
96°F (35.5°C)

NUMBER OF SPECIES: 3
ROBOROVSKI (ROBO),
CAMPBELL'S RUSSIAN,
WINTER WHITE RUSSIAN

WORLD'S TINIEST HEDGEHOG

Fourteen million years after an asteroid led to the extinction of most dinosaurs, the tiniest hedgehog to ever walk the Earth emerged. At just two inches (5 cm) long, *Silvacola acares* was only about the size of an adult human's thumb! Fossils of the hedgehog have been found in British Columbia, Canada, where *Silvacola acares* lived in a rainforest. *Silvacola acares*, whose name appropriately means "tiny forest dweller," was four times smaller than African pygmy hedgehogs, which are kept as pets today.

Researchers haven't been able to confirm from fossil evidence whether these half-pints had spines, like modern hedgehogs do. Larger hedgehogs from the same time period found in Europe had bristly hair, so it's possible these little fellas did, too. But to get a sense for just how small they were, chew on this: Their back teeth were the same size as three grains of salt! Scientists think the tiny hedgehogs ate insects and plants on the forest floor.

SILVACOLA ACARES

LIVED : 52 MILLION YEARS AGO, EOCENE EPOCH

SIZE: 2 INCHES (5 CM)

DIET: INSECTS, PLANTS

SILVACOLA HAD TINY TEETH! ITS BACK MOLARS WERE JUST .04 INCH (1 MM) LONG.

SMALL-AT-A-GLANCE

CHICKEN

DWARF RABBIT

1 SHORTEST FLIGHT

It doesn't seem possible, but chickens actually *can* fly ... sort of. They generally can't fly long or high enough to make it over a tall fence, but they can get a little air. Why the poor liftoff? Chickens have small wings compared to their body size, so the amateur aviators' proportions mean there isn't enough *oomph* to overcome their size when it comes to flight.

2 SHORTEST CANINE NOSE

A pug's short, squished, wrinkly snout certainly contributes to its signature look, but it also brings some trouble! Dogs regulate their temperature in part through their snout (that's why they have those wet noses!), and a pug's pushed-in nose isn't as efficient, which can cause it to overheat easily. (The same is true for other flat-faced dogs, like bulldogs and Boston terriers.)

3 SMALLEST RABBIT EARS

Dwarf rabbits are tiny, but it's their ears that are especially teensy. They stand straight up and can be as small as two inches (5 cm) long—the same length as a pink eraser. Not only do they detect sounds; they also help regulate their body temperature.

PUG

CHIHUAHUA

MOUSE

④ SMALLEST CANINE LITTER

Generally speaking, the smaller the dog, the smaller the litter of pups it'll have. Labrador retrievers are a large breed and average seven puppies per litter. But little Chihuahuas often have only one pup—and you can't get smaller than that!

⑤ SMALLEST SQUEEZE-THROUGH

Mice are the ultimate escape artists. Their flexible bodies allow them to squeeze through a crack the size of a dime! That means mice need to be kept in cages with very narrow slats—otherwise you'll be in for a game of hide-and-seek.

⑥ SHORTEST HAIRDO

Skinny pigs aren't actually pigs (they're guinea pigs), and they aren't necessarily "skinny"—they're just mostly hairless! The guinea pigs, which are hairless because of a genetic mutation, have tufts of hair on their nose, legs, and feet; otherwise they're smooth all over.

PERSONALITY-PREDICTOR HEAD-SCRATCHER

Here's an unexpected personality predictor: the shape of a dog's head! A recent study showed that dogs with certain head shapes were linked to certain types of behavior. "Brachycephalic" dogs—those with broad, wide skulls and short noses, like pugs, French bulldogs, and chow chows—tended to be more engaged and had a higher interest in playing with their humans.

SKINNY PIG

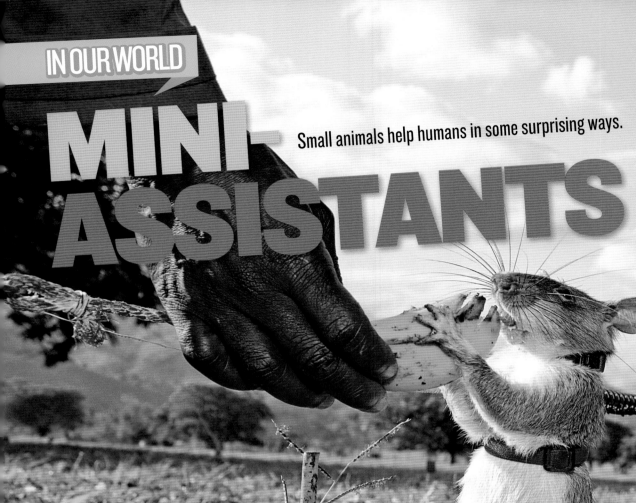

MINI-ASSISTANTS

Small animals help humans in some surprising ways.

A GROUP OF RATS IS CALLED A MISCHIEF.

n 1999, engineers at the U.S. Space Command at Peterson Air Force Base in Colorado Springs, Colorado, U.S.A., had a big problem. They needed to run wires for new computers at their missile warning center, but the wires had to go through narrow, 40-foot (12-m)-long tunnels that already had wires running through them! Luckily, their big problem had a small solution in the shape of Misty, a pet ferret. An officer at the base knew that ferrets were used to run wires in tight spaces in World War II airplanes, and he volunteered his pet for the job. After several trips that took Misty about an hour, she completed the job. For her efforts, Misty was awarded a strawberry Pop-Tart.

Ferrets aren't the only animals helping humans. Rats, with their small size and keen sense of smell, are helping save human lives in Africa. How? Land mines kill thousands of people a year in war-torn areas where they have been buried in the ground during conflict. Specially trained African giant pouched rats have worked in the African countries of Mozambique and Angola to sniff out the chemicals found in the land mines. When the rats locate a mine, they scratch the dirt above the location. And because these rats weigh less than 11 pounds (5 kg) each, they don't trigger the mine, which can then be defused, making everyone safer. What's in it for the rats? They get their favorite reward—bananas.

Match the tiny animal to the object or animal that's about the same size. How'd you do? Check the answer key to see if a (small) victory dance is in order.

HOW SMALL IS SMALL?

1

4

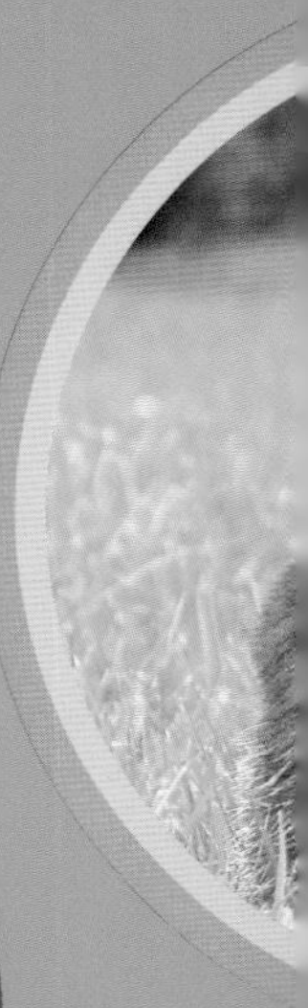

3

6

2

5

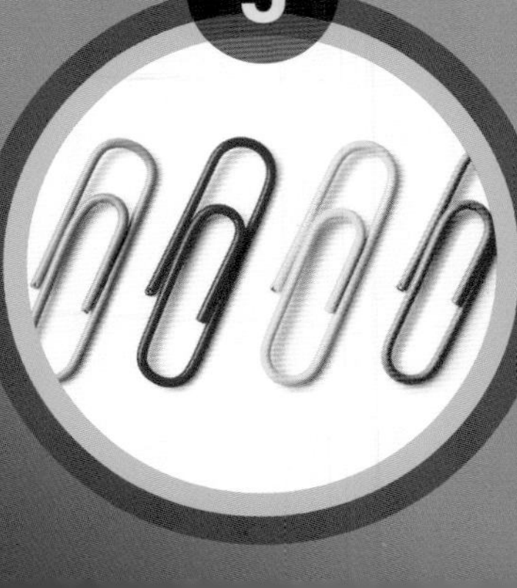

7

D

A

C

E

F

B

G

SMALLEST 65

CHAPTER 3

HOLD ON TO YOUR THINKING CAPS—THESE SMARTY PETS MIGHT JUST BLOW YOUR MIND.

OK, brainiacs: You know there are lots of different ways to measure smarts. So while these pets have all earned their place at the head of the class, there's still plenty of room for you to choose your own winners.

THE GOAT

This hoofed hotshot takes the top spot as our surprise winner. But don't let that get your goat! While goats have a reputation for being stubborn and unruly, those stereotypes overlook how inquisitive and intelligent these farm animals really are. Goats use their noggins to navigate living in complex social groups made up of kids (babies), moms, and dads. And researchers are just beginning to understand these four-legged Einsteins. Domesticated goats in one study solved a puzzle so they would be rewarded with a sweet treat, and on average it took them only 12 tries to master the problem. Then, when researchers retested them 10 months later, the goats quickly remembered the exact steps, getting to the fruit in less than two minutes. Some researchers think that goats may be as clever as dogs. Surprise!

SCIENTIFIC NAME: **CAPRA HIRCUS**

NUMBER OF BREEDS: **MORE THAN 200**

LIFE SPAN: **8 TO 12 YEARS OR LONGER**

WEIGHT: **UP TO 300 POUNDS (136 KG)**

BABY GOATS CAN STAND UP MINUTES AFTER **BEING BORN.**

FIRST DOMESTICATED:
10,000 YEARS AGO

NUMBER OF TEETH: **32**

HEIGHT OF FENCE NEEDED:
UP TO 5 FEET (1.5 M) FOR LARGER GOATS

THE RUNNERS-UP...

These bright animals take their place on the pet honor roll.

BRAINY BIRDS

PARAKEETS

These social birds are only about seven inches (18 cm) long. But don't let their small size fool you—these petite parrots are big in brain-power. Parakeets understand that if a bit of banana is hidden under a napkin, for example, that doesn't mean the treat has disappeared for good. They understand that objects continue to exist even if the objects can't be seen—a skill called object permanence, which human babies learn as well.

CLEVER RODENTS

RATS

Wild rats live in a wide variety of environments, such as rainforests, marshes, densely packed cities, and ships. These rodents create pathways around their environments to remember where to find food or to help them avoid trouble. It's no surprise that pet rats share the same brainy skills as their wild cousins. Once they learn a navigation route, they never forget it. No GPS needed for these clever critters!

DISTINGUISHED DOGS

POODLES

Elegant-looking and refined, poodles may seem like the aristocrats of the dog world. But these pups are more than primping prima donnas: A survey of dog-show judges puts poodles at the top of the list of smart breeds. Poodles were bred to retrieve game birds from the water, and it's in their nature to excel at learning commands. They've even been trained to form a conga line!

CAT CHAMPION

ABYSSINIANS

This runner-up puts the "curious" in "curious cat." Abyssinians are considered one of the smartest cat breeds—and for good reason. They like to explore their homes, nosing into nooks and craning into crannies. They also tend to be playful and social, earning the nickname "Aby-silly-an." Abys can be taught to walk on a leash.

These runners-up win accolades for specific smarty-pants skills.

HAPPY HOGS

PIGS

This runner-up is no mental slouch, even if it likes to slop around in the mud! Pigs possess brains way beyond the barnyard. In one study, pigs were trained to learn how to anticipate positive things, like getting chocolate-covered raisins from their humans, or a negative experience, like having to go into a time-out. When pigs that hadn't been trained were placed in the same pen as those that had, they quickly understood if a treat or a trick was coming by paying attention to the behavior of the pigs already in the study. Brilliant!

CLEVER FOWL

CHICKENS

Why did the chicken cross the road? If you think it might have noticed the green light, you could be right! Chickens know the difference between shapes and colors. These clever birds also can tell which of two groups has more objects in it, meaning they have a sense of numbers. And in a study testing willpower, chickens would hold off eating in the short term if they knew they would get more food later. They might have more willpower than your little brother!

SUPERIOR SLEUTHS

FERRETS

Master problem-solvers, these skillful mammals can ferret out (get it?) some problems better than cats or dogs can. Ferrets can open the latches of their enclosures, which can cause their humans some headaches, but they also can understand gestures. A study showed that if people pointed to a container that held tasty foods, ferrets quickly understood the meaning of that gesture.

TOUCH-SCREEN TITLEHOLDER

RED-FOOTED TORTOISE

Researchers taught four red-footed tortoises how to use a touch screen—and it wasn't just so they could send text messages! The scientists were testing the tortoises' memories. The animals learned that by touching a specific image on the screen, they would get a tasty reward of sweet corn, strawberry, or mushroom bits. They also figured out how to get strawberry bits at the end of each of eight sections of a maze without revisiting any part of the maze they had already been in.

PSYCHIC PETS

Cats may have a knack for batting around balls of yarn, but does that make them smart about soccer?

RUBBING A DRYER SHEET ON A DOG DURING AN ELECTRICAL STORM CAN CALM HIM.

This cat from Russia isn't known for his fancy footwork, but he does score points with the fans. Achilles, a deaf cat who lives in St. Petersburg's Hermitage Museum, became a celebrity for his ability to predict the winner of FIFA World Cup soccer matches in 2018. Achilles was presented with two bowls of food with a flag for each competing team in each bowl. Whichever bowl he chose to eat from was deemed Achilles's predicted winner of the upcoming game. Going into the final game, Achilles had a 75 percent prediction accuracy rate. Talk about the cat's meow! His caretakers believe that Achilles's deafness is an advantage: It allows him to make a prediction without distractions, they say.

So, is Achilles a bona fide fortune-teller? Some skeptical animal behavior experts say no. Besides Achilles, other animals—from a pig to a parakeet to an octopus—have accurately predicted the outcomes of World Cup games, but it's not because they've been keeping up on the teams' stats. Animals may have a preference for one side of their body, experts say, and therefore may choose food on the side that they favor (which may happen to be the winning team). Animals can also pick up on cues from people around them. If there is even a subtle indication that one side is preferred, based on a hand motion or a glance of the eye by a caretaker, an in-tune animal may choose a specific bowl (or flag). Animals may not be superfans, but they sometimes pay superclose attention!

WEATHER-PREDICTING PUPS

Are stormy skies ahead? Ask your dog! Dogs don't need a weather app to know if a thunderstorm is coming. Some have natural weather-predicting abilities. For starters, some dogs can sense a drop in barometric pressure—which may make them anxious, knowing from past experiences that it can bring loud thunder booms or cracks of lightning. Another storm indicator: static on their coats! Large dogs and dogs with long or thick coats can build up static electricity during a storm, which may give them a small shock when they touch a metal object.

For their smarts and superior instincts to help save their humans, these pet heroes are all medal winners.

ANIMAL RESCUE

DEVOTED **DOG**

PUPPY SAVES GIRL

When three-year-old Karina Chikitova and her puppy got lost in the woods outside a remote town in Siberia, Russia, her family feared the worst. After nine days of keeping Karina warm at night, her loyal puppy then traveled back to the village and led a search party to the tall grass where she had made a bed. That's one amazing pup.

KARINA WITH A STATUE COMMEMORATING HER RESCUE

FEARLESS **FRIEND**

BIRD ALERTS OWNER

When a fire started in Andrew Hardiek's house, in Avilla, Indiana, U.S.A., his pet cockatiel, Dylan, seemed to know just what to do. Dylan started squawking and wouldn't stop, which woke up Andrew from a deep sleep in time for him to save them both from the flames. That's some mighty know-how for such a tiny parrot!

PERSISTENT **FELINE**

CAT SUMMONS HELP

Janet Rawlinson's cat Slinky Malinki was known to be shy and aloof, but that was before Janet had a bad reaction to some medicine. Sensing something was wrong, the two-year-old tomcat alerted the neighbors in the village of Cornholme, England. First Slinky tried to annoy their dogs, and then the quick-thinking pet tapped on their window with his paw.

SUPER **SNIFFER**

HOUND DETECTS CANCER

When Lauren Gauthier, who lived in upstate New York, U.S.A., rescued an abandoned hunting hound—whom she named Victoria—she knew she had found a loyal friend ... but a literal lifesaving one? Who knew? Whenever Lauren would cuddle with Victoria, the pup would sniff a small spot on her human's nose. When Victoria kept sniffing even after the spot went away, Lauren figured she should have it looked at. Good thing: The spot was skin cancer, and the early detection saved her life.

QUICK-THINKING **KITTY**

CAT SAVES FAMILY

Luna the cat sensed something was wrong even though her family was fast asleep. So the little black cat started nipping and biting at her mom's feet until the pesky annoyance woke up Emily Chappell-Root. Once awake, Emily realized that her house in Chester, South Carolina, U.S.A., was on fire and that she needed to act fast. She got all six of her kids—and the family pets—outside to safety, thanks to this spunky kitty.

BRAVEST BREED

Snowstorm? No problem! Saint Bernards have helped save some 2,000 people, from lost kids to stranded soldiers. The snowy Saint Bernard Pass, a mountainous 49-mile (79-km) route between Italy and Switzerland in the Alps, has long been treacherous. Travelers would sometimes become disoriented during bad snowstorms or get buried by monstrous avalanches or 40-foot (12-m)-tall snow drifts. Monks living in the isolated region started using these working dogs in the mid-1700s to locate missing or injured trekkers. The massive dogs would go out in teams, with one dog staying with travelers to keep them safe and warm and the other heading back to alert rescuers. With smarts, stamina, and an excellent sense of direction, Saint Bernards are truly rescue stars.

THE AMAZING ACRO-CATS

Introducing Chicago's Cat Circus!

Unlike dogs, cats aren't usually up for performing tricks. They like to do things on their own terms. But there's a troupe of cats from Chicago, Illinois, U.S.A., that jump through hoops, climb up ropes, and even roll balls with their front paws! The Amazing Acro-Cats are a group of a dozen orphaned and rescued cats that their handler (and ringleader), Samantha Martin, takes on a custom tour bus to perform across the United States.

The Amazing Acro-Cats are clicker-trained, meaning that they learn to respond to the sound of a clicker that Martin holds in her hand. (They also get lots of treats.) The cats ride skateboards, ring bells, walk on a high wire, and even push a tiny shopping cart. But sometimes kitties will be kitties, and the Acro-Cats will occasionally get distracted during a performance and wander into the audience or decide to take a grooming break. Some of the cats are outright rock stars, playing in a band called the Rock Cats. The kitties play drums, keyboard, and even a cowbell, sometimes in *purr*-fect harmony.

TEACHING THE CLICKER METHOD

The Amazing Acro-Cats are taught their tricks through the clicker method. In the early stages of their training, the cats learn that the sound of a click is associated with a special treat. Next, their handler waits for them to perform a certain behavior that she wants them to do, like sit. When they sit, she clicks the clicker and gives them a treat. Over time, the cats learn that if they hear the click and do what they're supposed to do, they get a reward. This is called positive reinforcement.

PARROTS ARE THE ONLY BIRDS THAT CAN FEED THEMSELVES WITH THEIR FEET.

CHATTY BIRD

Parrots are expert talkers.

Better watch what you say around a parrot—you may never hear the end of it! Parrots are vocal learners, which means they can figure out how to imitate sounds, including people's conversations. How do they do it?

Parrots' throat structure is similar to humans', and they have long, muscular tongues that they use to modify sounds. Plus, parrots' brains are structured differently from other birds'; they have defined parts that control vocal learning that other birds don't. Parrots are social and like to fit in with their flock, and to do that they make a lot of noise. When they're around only people, humans are their flock, so they try to keep up.

But when parrots talk, do they know what they're saying? Yes and no. They associate certain things with words but not deeper meaning. When you walk into a room, your pet parrot might say, "Hello! How are you?" She is probably mimicking the phrase she's heard before, but unfortunately, she is not truly wondering how your day is going. That's not to say that parrots don't have plenty of things to talk about. One African gray parrot named Prudle was so good at mimicking that he had a vocabulary of 1,000 words!

ALEX, THE EXCEPTIONALLY SMART PARROT

An African gray parrot named Alex took talking to the next level. Alex not only mimicked; he also learned to identify objects with words. During his 31-year life, he learned to identify 50 objects, seven colors, and five shapes. He could also understand the concept of "bigger" and "smaller." Alex even invented his own terms: When he was given a cake for his birthday, he called it "yummy bread"!

BATTLE OF WITS

Which pet is the bigger brainiac?

TORTOISE vs. RAT

WINNER

BEST DECISION-MAKER

Tortoises may not be swift, but when it comes to making decisions, they are quick thinkers. British scientist Anna Wilkinson's pet red-footed tortoise outsmarted rats in 2006 when put to the test in a maze, more efficiently remembering paths it had taken.

DOG vs. CAT

BEST BRAINPOWER

This may get pet owners fighting like cats and dogs, but a 2017 study by six different universities in the United States, Brazil, Denmark, and South Africa revealed that dogs have twice as many neurons—the brain's information processing units—as cats do. Does that make them twice as smart? Not exactly, but researchers think their increased brainpower makes them capable of more complex and flexible behavior.

WINNER

BEST PROBLEM-SOLVER

Donkeys don't horse around when it comes to solving problems. In 2013, British researchers tested both horses' and donkeys' abilities at finding an opening in a gate to get to food. Donkeys may be stubborn, but they beat out the horses every time.

WINNER

DONKEY vs. HORSE

SMARTEST PIG

Sorry, guinea pigs, but you can't squeak out a win here. As one of the few animals that can recognize themselves in a mirror, pigs are definitely smarty-pants. Kids can't even do that until around age two! Scientists have found that pigs even show an understanding of how mirrors work and can use the reflections to find food.

GUINEA PIG vs. PIG

WINNER

BIRD vs. LIZARD

WINNER

BEST TEST-TAKER

Reptiles don't get a lot of credit for smarts. But in one 2011 study, anoles (a type of lizard often kept as pets) proved to be smarter than most birds in a series of tests to find a hidden worm. The anoles even changed up their technique when they were presented with a new problem.

BRAIN POWER

It makes sense that bigger animals would have larger brains, but does that mean bigger is always better? Not quite. Scientists are learning that when it comes to smarts, it's how the different parts of the brain work together that can make the difference, even in a small brain. See how these pet brains compare in relative size to some common items.

BEAGLE

a tangerine =

GOLDFISH = a grain of sand

RAT

a green grape = GUINEA PIG

= four raisins

a kiwi-fruit = CAT

a grape-fruit = PIG

an apple = HORSE

an unshelled walnut = BLUE-AND-YELLOW MACAW

LASSIE:
THE CLEVEREST
ON-SCREEN COLLIE

assie always saved the day. As the star of books, movies, and television, the lovable collie could always be counted on to lend a helping paw to her humans. Through her cleverness and resourcefulness, she earned a place in the hearts of her fans—and showed them how capable a canine could be.

The adventures of Lassie began with a short story, written in 1938, about a dog whose intelligence and sensitivity were humanlike. Lassie, who was beloved for her smarts and courage, was always portrayed as a female, but the dogs who played her on-screen were male—all descendants of the original Lassie actor, whose name was Pal. (Male collies were chosen because they are larger and don't seasonally shed as much as females.) The well-trained dog actors and adept editing by the filmmakers made Lassie appear to be capable of doing just about anything—from knocking down criminals to leaping out of windows to make a daring rescue. But that's not to say that Lassie wasn't bright. The dogs who played Lassie knew over 100 commands!

"LASSIE" HAS A STAR ON THE HOLLYWOOD WALK OF FAME!

MORE CELEBRITY PUPS

Lassie wasn't Hollywood's only bright canine star. Rin Tin Tin, a German shepherd who in real life was rescued by a U.S. soldier on a battlefield in France during World War I, went on to star in 27 films! The golden retriever who played a hoopster in the movie *Air Bud* was a stray dog whose adopted owner taught him to dunk a ball, which got him his acting job. And then there's Toto, the pup that Dorothy carried in a basket in *The Wizard of Oz*. Casting for this role was the reverse of Lassie's: On-screen Toto was portrayed as a male, but the dog was in fact played by a female named Terry.

RIN TIN TIN

TOTO

AIR BUD

SMART-AT-A-GLANCE

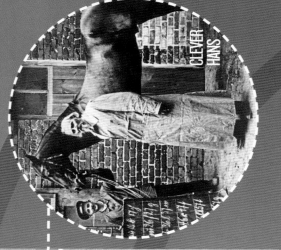

CLEVER HANS

LLAMA

CAT

1 CLEVEREST HORSE

In the late 19th century, a performance horse named Clever Hans began wowing crowds by responding to his handler's questions with hoof taps. It appeared that Clever Hans could perform basic math, tell time, and spell. Later it was discovered that the horse was responding to very subtle (probably unintentional) cues from his handler about what answers to give. Still, Hans's attentiveness is nothing to neigh at!

2 BEST CAT NAVIGATOR

A cat named Holly who got lost while on vacation with her owners in Florida, U.S.A., managed to find her way home 60 days later ... after a nearly 200-mile (322-km) walk! While most animals have a good sense of direction, Holly's GPS-like abilities are next-level.

3 SMARTEST WATCH "DOG"

Who better to guard your flock of sheep than an expert kicker and spitter? In Colorado, U.S.A., some sheep ranchers use llamas rather than dogs to protect their sheep from coyotes. Llamas aren't afraid of the coyotes, and when llamas are disturbed, they make loud sounds that send the predators running.

CHICKEN

SMARTEST LOCK-PICKER

Watch your valuables around Goffin's cockatoos! Scientists put a group of them to the test to see how well they could open a box with five different types of locks. After some trial and error, the feathered locksmiths figured out how to unlock each one for a treat.

4

SMARTEST WARNING SIGNAL

Chickens' communication is far more complicated than *cluck-cluck*. They have two dozen different vocalizations, including one that lets the rest of the flock know that a ground predator is near and a different one that warns of a flying predator, like a hawk in the air.

5

SMARTEST DOGGIE DOOR

Doggie doors are convenient for letting your pup come and go as she pleases, but they're not convenient when uninvited guests show up in your house! You can now buy a "smart pet door" that knows to let only your dog (or cat) into the house. A special chip is attached to your pet's collar, giving her the exclusive on the open-door policy.

6

COCKATOO

DOG

THE ANTERNET!

Ants can tell us a lot about computer networks.

ANTS DON'T HAVE EARS.

Dozens and dozens of ants scurry through sand tunnels in an ant farm. It can be mesmerizing to watch these six-legged creatures traveling to and fro. They look pretty busy, but how do they know where to go and what to do?

Ants live in large colonies, but there's no big boss handing out orders. Instead, ants share information using social networks. They figure out what needs to be done by touching antennae together and by following chemical trails. When researchers started looking at ant society, they realized something: Just like an ant farm, the internet also operates as a giant hub of activity without a central "boss." Researchers at Stanford University in California, U.S.A., dubbed just such a network of harvester ants in Arizona, U.S.A., the "Anternet."

Are these ants using the internet to communicate? No, that's silly. But they share information in ways similar to how data is regulated as it travels across interconnected networks—and they've been doing it for millions of years! Here's what the scientists found. Some harvester ants, which live in dry deserts, go out to search for seeds to eat. But when it's superhot, the ants can get dehydrated quickly, which is dangerous. Since they don't want to be caught outside, they regulate the flow of ants into and out of the nest and wait until conditions improve to go searching for seeds. In a similar way, information being sent on the internet is slowed down if there isn't enough bandwidth to handle it. Scientists are studying ant networks to see what ants can teach us about making the human world more efficient, from online gaming systems to trucks delivering goods. What else can these import-*ant* creatures—with more than 12,000 species—teach us?

SOME ANT
QUEENS
CAN LIVE
FOR **30**
YEARS.

ANTS CAN CARRY
UP TO **50** TIMES
THEIR BODY WEIGHT.

With a little time and patience, you can train your pup to do this basic trick.

TEACH YOUR DOG HOW TO **WAVE**

If your dog knows how to sit and shake "hands," he is well on his way to learning how to give you a friendly wave. Here's how to teach him:

1

FIND A PLACE TO DO YOUR TRAINING THAT IS FREE OF DISTRACTION. And make sure you have some treats on hand.

2

ASK YOUR DOG TO SIT, and then give him the command to "shake." When he lifts his paw to shake hands, move your hand a little higher than normal, so he has to reach up a bit. After he successfully moves his paw up farther than he would for a shake, give him a treat and tell him good job.

3

REPEAT THIS SEVERAL TIMES and each time raise your hand a little bit higher, until eventually he reaches his paw above his head. Make sure to praise him and give him a treat each time.

4

GIVE HIM THE COMMAND FOR "SHAKE" AGAIN, shake his paw, and give him a treat. This will help him reset and learn that there is a difference between shaking hands and waving.

Note: Training sessions should be nice and short, just a few minutes at a time, and just a few times during the day. If your dog is frustrated or distracted, move on to a more familiar command and try again later. Never scold your dog if he isn't getting it right. Be patient, and eventually your waving pooch will be the friendliest dog on the block!

5

THEN PUT YOUR HAND UP HIGH AGAIN AND GIVE HIM THE COMMAND "WAVE."
Do this over and over, making sure his paw is above his head before giving him a treat and praising him. In no time, he will be lifting his paw above his head for a friendly wave, without your hand being there!

SMARTEST 93

CHAPTER 4

THESE PETS ARE NOT JUST WONDERFUL— THEY'RE ALSO WONDERFULLY WEIRD.

From rodents that like dust baths to weasels that like to dance, the winners in this chapter are far from typical—but that just makes them all the more marvelous.

THE TARANTULA

Not too many pets can regrow their legs. Or molt (shed their exoskeletons) periodically. Or replace their internal organs. For these reasons and more (there are more?!), tarantulas scurry into the weird winners' circle.

These eight-legged beauties—spiders with hairy bodies—also come with an assortment of oddball defense mechanisms. Some tarantulas flick sharp, barb-tipped hairs (called urticating hairs) from their abdomens when threatened. In the wild, these hairs can get into the eyes or noses of attacking predators, sending them packing. Tarantulas also bite with sharp fangs, which can feel like a bee sting. And they secrete digestive chemicals that liquefy their prey so they can suck them up! Though much loved by their owners, tarantulas are "look but don't touch" pets.

SIZE: 4.75 INCHES (12 CM) LONG

LEG SPAN: UP TO 11 INCHES (28 CM)

SCIENTIFIC NAME: _THERAPHOSIDAE_

LIFE SPAN: UP TO 30 YEARS IN THE WILD

NUMBER OF SPECIES: MORE THAN 900

TARANTULAS CAN REGROW LOST LEGS.

NUMBER OF FEEDINGS
PER WEEK: **1 OR 2**

LENGTH OF FANGS: **.75 INCH (2 CM)**

NAME FOR IMMATURE SPIDERS:
SPIDERLINGS

These weird winners will have you doing a double take!

CRAZIEST COSTUME

VEILED CHAMELEON

Here's a riddle for you: What has hundreds of different looks but no need for a wardrobe? The veiled chameleon, that's what! This hardy reptile can change its skin color from orange and yellow to green to black and blue. It can also form different colorful patterns of spots and stripes. In the wild, chameleons live in vegetated areas of the Arabian Peninsula, where they make their homes in trees, in village gardens, and even along roadways.

BALD **BEAUTY**

SPHYNX

This kitty never has to worry about a bad hair day! The breed has been around only since 1966, when the first known hairless kitten was born in Toronto, Canada, to two fully haired parents. These sweet and mischievous cats have loose, wrinkly skin on their faces, which makes them look wise beyond their years. These smooth-skin felines seek out sunny spots to sleep, and the fine hairs on the sphynx's body can make the cat feel like a warm, fuzzy peach. Awww!

MOP **TOP**

KOMONDOR

No need to be embarrassed if you mistake this winner for a mop. The komondor's kooky look comes from the white corded hair that covers its body, which means this breed can easily be confused with a mass of white rope. A thousand years ago, nomadic Magyars brought the dog to Hungary, their native land, to protect flocks of sheep. Their distinctive coat protects against bad weather—and the sharp teeth of wolves looking for a sheeplike snack.

SUPER **SNOUT**

ÇATALBURUN

This dog wins for its unusual-looking snout. The çatalburun is one of only a few dog breeds with a split nose. *Çatalburun* even means "fork nose" in its native Turkey! The medium-size hunting dog is both a loyal companion and an agile hunter.

MORE RUNNERS-UP...

These atypical pets have some amazingly unusual attributes.

WINNING **WHISKERS**

BRISTLENOSE PLECO

These spotted suckerfish look like something straight out of the Jurassic. But bristlenose plecos and their whiskery snouts are definitely at home in the 21st century. These armored catfish originate in the Amazon and have an added bonus trait: The five-inch (13-cm)-long fish like to eat algae that grow in their freshwater tanks, so they function as a tank cleaner. Score!

HEAD **HONCHO**

LESSER SULPHUR-CRESTED COCKATOO

The striking yellow feathers on the head of this small cockatoo certainly grab some attention. But that's not the only way this bird commands respect. When cockatoos speak, they can be very loud ... and they need to be! In the wild, these tropical birds live in dark forests. They want to be heard, because it isn't a sure thing they will be seen—even with their memorable headdress.

MASTER **MIMIC**

WESTERN HOGNOSE SNAKE

While its mesmerizing coat colors and upturned nose helped this scaly creature secure the win, its mimicking behavior is what makes this snake really strange. When threatened, western hognose snakes flatten out their necks to appear to be a cobra, and then they make hissing sounds and rattles to mimic a rattlesnake. While harmless, this cold-blooded pet will even strike at threats (but with a closed mouth) and then play dead. Western hognose snakes can be tricky to care for, so first-time snake owners might consider a more beginner-friendly breed.

CHAMPION **CROAKER**

PAC-MAN FROG

A pet frog named after a video game—winner! This wild-looking amphibian, also known as a horned frog, lives in the humid tropical forests of South America. But instead of eating computer dots, these frogs munch on crickets, worms, and even mice. Fill the bottom of a Pac-Man habitat with shredded coconut husks and watch as these frogs burrow into the stuff.

WRINKLY
DOGS

This creased breed is among the most ancient on Earth.

ADULT SHAR-PEI

SHAR-PEI ARE ONE OF ONLY TWO BREEDS OF DOGS TO HAVE A BLUE-BLACK TONGUE. (THE OTHER IS THE CHOW CHOW.)

There's nothing like wrinkles to give off the vibe of wisdom. And *these* wrinkles are thousands of years in the making! Shar-pei—whose creased countenance gives their eyes a sunken, soulful look—date back 2,000 years to China's Han dynasty. They were used for hunting, herding, and guarding livestock.

Shar-pei are best known for their furrowed brows and loose skin, but wrinkles aren't their only unusual feature. They also have a hippopotamus-shaped muzzle and tiny triangular ears. Wonder what those wrinkles feel like to pet? A shar-pei's coat is not smooth, that's for sure! In fact, *shar-pei* translates from the Chinese as "sand skin"—because the fur feels like sandpaper! Shar-pei puppies tend to have wrinkles all over. But when they grow up, they grow into their skin, and eventually most have wrinkles only on their head. Shar-pei are the opposite of humans: For them, *losing* their wrinkles is a sign of getting older!

ALL THOSE WRINKLES CAN BE PROBLEMATIC! OWNERS OF WRINKLY DOGS HAVE TO TAKE EXTRA CARE TO MAKE SURE THE NOOKS AND CRANNIES ARE KEPT CLEAN.

SUPERSTITION STANDOUTS

The odd ideas behind some common animal tales.

KITTY KARMA

CATS

If a black cat crosses your path, watch out! Or maybe not. The idea that black cats bring bad luck most likely came from an old belief that black cats were witches in disguise. But don't fear: Black cats aren't going to bring you bad luck—though not watching where you walk just might.

NO SUCH LUCK

DOGS

Nobody wants to step in, um, a dog's mess. But in France, there is a silver lining. It's believed that if you accidentally step in poop with your left foot, you'll have good luck!

104

HOWLING **HARBINGER**
DOGS

When a dog howls, you might think it just wants to be let out. But some people think it is an omen that means death is lurking about. Does the dog know something we don't? Probably not. More than likely, the loud pooch is howling because he or she is lonely.

POSITIVE **POOP**
BIRDS

You're having fun with your friends outside when a bird decides to go to the bathroom on your head. Yuck! But some people think that isn't a bad thing after all. Instead, they see a little bird "hair gel" as a positive event—and one that will bring good luck. Go figure!

THAT'S **HARE-BRAINED!**
RABBITS

When the first of the month comes around, some people say the words "rabbit, rabbit" or "white rabbits" to bring them good luck. What gives? The superstition traces back to the early 20th century in England; from there it made its way to New England. If you forget, that's OK; you can just say "black rabbit" or "tibbar" (that's "rabbit" backward, of course).

TOKYO CAT CAFÉ

Enter a fairy-tale world full of cats!

Once considered wacky, cat cafés have become the norm in Tokyo, Japan. There are dozens scattered around the city, most with the aim of allowing customers to sit and enjoy a cup of tea or coffee with a cat purring quietly nearby. Sounds simple enough. But one Tokyo café has taken the experience to the next level!

At Cat Café Temari no Ouchi, the theme is "mysterious cat forest." Visitors spend time in this indoor wonderland full of fabricated tree stumps (perfect for a cat to perch on), hollowed-out logs, and cottages that look to be lifted straight from the pages of "Hansel and Gretel." Once you pay admission to enter the café, you can stay and lounge with the kitties as long as you'd like. Drinks for the humans are available and include "fluffy coffee," a latte with a paw print swirled into the foam on top.

Twenty cats are full-time residents. If they get tired of being around people, they can opt to head off to a "staff only" section, where they can have some quiet time. The cats can be petted, but for their safety, they shouldn't be picked up by customers. The staff prefers that the kitties make their own choices—which usually involves a lot of snoozing.

NOT A CAT PERSON? HOP ON OVER TO THIS CAFÉ

Cat cafés are just one of many pet-themed cafés in Japan. Among the most popular? Rabbit cafés. At Mimi, a bunny café in Tokyo, the rabbits are free to hop around as they please, playing with one another and getting cuddles from visitors. They're also ready to eat snacks; upon entry, each visitor gets a bowl of treats to feed the rabbits. About 30 rabbits call the café home, but only about 10 are let out to mingle at a time. The others are rotated in so that all the bunnies get a proper mix of hop and quiet time.

STINKY, BENDY, DANCING FERRETS!

There's nothing ordinary about a ferret.

For starters, ferrets are smelly. A member of the weasel family (lump them in with skunks, weasels, and otters), ferrets have a scent gland under their tail, similar to that of a skunk. They release an odor when they are excited, angry, or scared. Spaying or neutering them helps reduce the smell, but they will always maintain a very slight musky odor. It's just their natural perfume.

Next up is their extreme flexibility! Thanks to extra-long vertebrae, ferrets have long and bendy bodies with rather short legs. This makes them experts at wiggling through tight spaces—whether they're tunnels out in the wild or plastic tubes in the house. It's no surprise that they are also extreme escape artists. Owners must make sure the gaps in their enclosure are less than an inch (2.5 cm) wide; otherwise they'll stretch like a rubber band and wiggle on out!

Ferrets are individuals even when it comes to how they vocalize. Some make lots of sounds, and others are quiet as mice. If they're feeling playful, some might make a chuckling or chattering noise. Some hiss as their regular form of communication, and others hiss to say, "Back off." Regardless of a ferret's personality, a screaming sound from a ferret is never a good thing: It means it is afraid or in pain.

And finally, ferrets can dance—the kind of dancing that is guaranteed to go viral. When ferrets feel playful, they arch their back, puff their tail, and move side to side. Cue the music and keep the camera rolling!

AND WITH A SNEAKY SIDE, TOO!

There's a reason that the word "ferret" is derived from the Latin word *furittus*, which means "thief." Ferrets are known for taking things that aren't theirs! As part of their nesting instinct, ferrets are natural hoarders. Ferret pet owners often report that the little pickpockets like to steal small objects and hide them away!

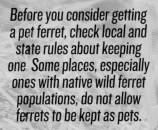

Before you consider getting a pet ferret, check local and state rules about keeping one. Some places, especially ones with native wild ferret populations, do not allow ferrets to be kept as pets.

BATTLE OF THE WEIRDEST

Which pet will win in these wacky matchups?

WINNER

DUST VS. SALIVA

WEIRDEST BATH

Cats spend up to 25 percent of their waking hours cleaning and grooming their fur with their tongues. (The saliva not only cleans kitties but also lowers their body temperature.) That may not sound like your idea of a luxurious bath, but chinchillas take fur maintenance to a whole other level. These rodents have one of the lushest coats of any animal, but they can keep it clean only with regular baths in ... dust. The dust baths, which they should take several times a week, help remove oil from their coat.

MOST UNUSUAL YARN

What more could a crafter need than a homegrown supply of yarn and felt! Some people spin their own dogs' fur into a product called chiengora, or dog yarn. It takes at least a garbage bag full of fur to spin a ball of yarn like you'd buy in the store, and then you're ready to knit! Other crafters turn their cats' fur into felt. One Japanese artist felts her cats' fur into hats that her cats then wear.

DOG FUR VS. CAT FUR

TIE

WINKING vs. LEANING

WINNER

WACKIEST SIGN OF RELAXATION

You know you're bonded with your dog when she leans on you—quite literally! When a calm, relaxed dog leans into your leg, it means she trusts you. But nothing says "no worries" quite like a wink. A relaxed, trusting kitty with droopy eyes will give you a blink—and even wink—called a "kitty kiss." Aww!

YODEL vs. SNEEZE

WEIRDEST SOUND

What better way to alert your friends that there's danger approaching than to ... sneeze? An achoo is exactly what a goat uses when it senses danger. A sneeze is sweet, but a little subtle. Basenjis, a type of hound dog, don't sneeze, and they don't even bark. Instead, they let out a sound best described as a yodel to express themselves! Why sneeze when you can sing it loud?

WINNER

WEIRDEST HABITS

Sometimes after your pup poops, you might find him kicking up grass. Why the happy feet? He's marking his territory. Dogs have glands in their feet that secrete special chemicals called pheromones. Scraping the ground is their way of claiming their turf. Those same chemicals are at play when your cat rubs her cheeks on the furniture, your legs, or trees. By laying down a scent, she is claiming the house—and you—as her own. While both dogs and cats have the same motive, cats win for being less messy about it!

CHEEK RUBS vs. HIGH KICKS

WINNER

LUXE LIFE

Humans spoil their pets with some seriously posh products!

Lifeguard stand dog house
$9,900

Barrington birdhouse
$3,000

Royal dog bed
$443.20

Cat perfume
$90

Louis Vuitton pet carrier
$3,550

Pet treadmill
$2,717

AN ANCIENT EGYPTIAN CAT
STATUE, REPRESENTING
THE GODDESS BASTET

ANCIENT EGYPTIAN PETS:
FROM CROCS TO CATS

Ancient Egyptians really liked their pets. They kept company with some of the animals we do today, like dogs, who were used for hunting and guarding. But some of their companions were a bit more unusual (like falcons and monkeys), and some were *really* unusual (like hippos and crocodiles)! Hippos showed one's power and wealth. Crocodiles were kept to represent Sobek, the crocodile god. Crocodiles were a danger to Egyptians living near rivers and waterways, and having one as a pet displayed the owner's strength.

One of the most common Egyptian pets was also the most revered. It is believed most Egyptian households had a pet cat, which was useful in helping keep the home clear of pests like rats and snakes. But cats were also held in high esteem because the Egyptian goddess Bastet was worshipped in the form of half cat, half woman. Cats were held in such high regard that when a family's cat died, everyone in the household shaved their eyebrows in mourning.

A HIPPO STATUE FROM ANCIENT EGYPT

ANIMALS IN THE AFTERLIFE

Ancient Egyptian pets weren't just a part of everyday life. They were portrayed in paintings on tomb walls and were even mummified after their death and included in their owners' tombs to accompany them in the afterlife. Other animals were mummified and presented to the gods as a sacred offering. Besides cats, dogs, crocodiles, monkeys, and baboons, archaeologists have found small mummified animals, like fish, lizards, and even beetles. Archaeologists have found dozens of catacombs (underground cemeteries) in Egypt containing millions of mummified animals. In 2018, during an excavation of a 4,500-year-old Egyptian tomb near Cairo, dozens of mummified cats, as well as 100 gilded wood cat statues, were found.

WEIRD-AT-A-GLANCE

ASIATIC BLACK BEAR

TIBETAN MASTIFF

MAREMMA

CORGIPOO

1 WEIRDEST PET MIX-UP

A family in China thought they had adopted a Tibetan mastiff puppy, but it turned out to be an Asiatic black bear! The "dog's" huge appetite and fast growth made them suspicious. Wildlife professionals confirmed it was indeed a bear and took it in under their care.

2 WEIRDEST HYBRID NAME

From labradoodle (a Labrador retriever–poodle mix) to chug (a Chihuahua–pug mix), there are lots of silly names for mixed-breed dogs. But this one might get the biggest giggles: the corgipoo! That's a mix between a corgi and a poodle.

3 WEIRDEST DOG JOB

Penguins and dogs don't usually hang out together, but on one small island off Australia, dogs were the ultimate heroes to a colony of penguins. The penguins were being overhunted by foxes, so a farmer sent one of his dogs to help out. Maremma dogs are trained to guard livestock, so protecting penguins came naturally to Oddball, the first of several Maremmas brought to the island to stop the fox attacks. The penguin-protecting pups ultimately saved the colony.

PEACOCK

4. WEIRDEST FORM OF AFFECTION

When they are relaxed, African gray parrots sometimes shrink the pupils of their eyes and then open them up again—a behavior called "pinning." It means they are happy. And if they regurgitate food in front of you, it means they like you!

5. WEIRDEST BODY LANGUAGE

Here's one way to know how a horse feels: Look at its ears. When both ears are turned to the side, it's relaxed. When it flicks one ear back, it is listening behind it. And when it pins both back, it's angry.

6. WEIRDEST PET TO TAKE ON A PLANE

Well, this isn't your typical carry-on luggage! A woman in New Jersey, U.S.A., tried to board a plane with her pet peacock. The bird was denied, in part because it didn't meet the guidelines for weight and size, the airline said.

AFRICAN GRAY PARROT

HORSE

CAT EYES MAKE ROADS SAFER.

A ROAD REFLECTOR
BASED ON PERCY
SHAW'S CAT EYE
DESIGN

This story begins on a dark, foggy road in 1933. Percy Shaw, a British inventor, was driving down a twisty road in Boothtown, England, when his car headlights reflected off the eyes of a cat that was sitting on the side of the road. (That's how the story goes, at least. Shaw never commented on it—maybe the cat got his tongue?) He not only avoided hitting the cat but also discovered he was driving down the wrong side of the road ... and was close to driving off a cliff! Other drivers may have been thankful for their good luck and carried on their way. But not Percy Shaw. He realized that the dark roads weren't safe and that maybe cats could help. How?

When you look into a cat's eyes at night, they glow. For Shaw, this led to a eureka moment. Because cats hunt during dawn and dusk, when light is low, they have a special layer of reflective cells in their eyes (called the tapetum lucidum) that captures more of the light and helps them see through the darkness. Shaw started experimenting with a road-safety device that would reflect the light from a car's headlights. His "cat's eyes" road markers use reflecting glass beads encased in a rubber housing placed inside a protective iron box. When this invention is put on the road, drivers can see the glow from these "cat's eyes" from 295 feet (90 m) ahead, which gives them about three seconds to react. Today, new designs give drivers even more time to react. Some styles use LED lights and different colors to warn of road conditions or contain small cameras to keep watch on the road. Now that's definitely the cat's meow!

PERCY SHAW

AN LED REFLECTOR

TO TEST HIS DESIGNS, PERCY SHAW WOULD DIG UP ROADWAYS WITHOUT PERMISSION.

HOST A WACKY PET CONTEST

Here's one way to celebrate the wild and crazy side of your pet: Host a pet contest in which the weirdest is the winner!

1

SPREAD THE WORD

First get the OK from your parents to hold the contest. Once you have the thumbs-up, send out invitations to your neighbors or a group of friends announcing your contest. For example:

TAKE A WALK ON THE WILD SIDE! Enter your pup in a weirdly wonderful fashion show! Wacky, creative costumes encouraged! Saturday at 2 p.m.

CALLING ALL TALENTED PETS! Put your best paw forward—whether it's dancing across the stage in a Hawaiian shirt or yodeling a tune. In this contest, weird wins!

2

SET THE STAGE
Use an old tablecloth as a
"red carpet" to roll out. Make
signs. And have some props
on hand for friends who might
need inspiration for their pets.
Pull out some lawn chairs for a
proper audience—and ask the
grown-ups to attend the
big show. (The more
applause, the better!)

3

**LIGHTS, CAMERA,
ACTION!**
Help your pets take center
stage. Walk them down the
red carpet or help them
perform a silly trick. Make
sure to have treats on hand
for the pets for a
job well done.

*Remember, if your pet
isn't up for performing,
don't force him. It's all
for fun, and pets should
never feel any pressure
to perform (or dress up) if
they don't want to.*

4

PHOTO OPPORTUNITY
Once the show is over, have a
homemade photo booth ready
to capture the fun of the day. A
few props—like bunny ears or
a mustache on a stick—and a
poster-board sign advertising
your show are all you need to
make a snapshot of the
memorable day.

WEIRDEST 121

CHAPTER 5

THINGS ARE ABOUT TO GET OFF-THE-CHARTS ADORABLE!

These cute pets have oodles of charm, bucketloads of charisma, and supersweet looks that will inspire more than a few *awwws*.

THE RAGDOLL CAT

FIRST BRED: 1960s

SIZE: 10–20 POUNDS (4.5–9 KG)

COAT LENGTH: SEMI-LONGHAIR

COLOR AT BIRTH: WHITE

A cat that doesn't mind being carried around like a doll? Now that's cute. But the ragdoll takes home the blue ribbon mostly because of its adorable mug and affectionate nature. These friendly felines play fetch, cozy up with their humans for a nap, and have been known to greet their owners at the door. The lovey-dovey breed gets its name from how the kitties turn floppy—kind of like a ragdoll—when being held and cuddled. These gentle lap cats will even make friends with the dogs in their families, earning them the nickname "puppy cats." Ragdolls are lovebugs through and through, so we awarded them our top spot. Sweet!

AGE WHEN COAT IS AT FULL COLOR: 3 YEARS

POSSIBLE COLORS AT ADULTHOOD: SEAL, BLUE, CHOCOLATE, LILAC, RED, OR CREAM

RAGDOLLS LOVE THE SOUND OF RUNNING WATER.

CATTITUDE: LAID-BACK AND GENTLE

These award winners are supercharged with charm.

CUTEST **HAIRDO**

ALPACA

With pointy ears and soft, round faces, these gentle herd animals take the cake for cuteness. Alpacas' soft, fine fleece makes this member of the camelid family (which includes llamas and, yes, camels) feel like a big teddy bear. Alpacas, which were domesticated thousands of years ago in the mountains of South America from wild vicuñas, have been delighting people for ages.

PORTUGUESE WATER DOG

Portuguese water dogs are not just supercute. They also sport a coat of ringlets that won't cause the achoos: Because Porties don't shed their hair, the pups are hypoallergenic. Cute and sniffle free? Score! The muscular dog was bred to work on fishing boats off the coast of Portugal, and today Porties are still used for water rescues.

DAINTY DARLING

LIONHEAD RABBIT

The name of these long-haired bunnies might fool you into thinking they belong on the African savanna. But don't fall for it: Lionhead rabbits got their name from the two-inch (5-cm)-long "manes" surrounding their charming faces. Weighing about three pounds (1.4 kg), these little cottontails aren't kings of the jungle, but they do make perfect pets.

LOVELY **LIZARD**

LEOPARD GECKO

Leapin' lizards, that's a cute smile! With their wide snouts, leopard geckos look like they are perpetually grinning. Geckos come in a wide variety of cool patterns and bright colors, way beyond the simple spots that gave this reptile its name. In the wild, these lizards live in arid parts of Asia and the Middle East. But don't expect them to climb the walls: Unlike some other geckos, they have claws instead of sticky toe pads.

MORE RUNNERS-UP...

In the barnyard battle for cuteness, these petite prizewinners come out on top.

FUZZY FOWL

DUCKLING

These yellow fluffs of cuteness waddle their way into our hearts. Ducklings are born with the instinct to follow their moms immediately after hatching, a trait that's known as imprinting. That is why it's common to see a string of ducklings following behind their mama. It helps keep the youngsters safe and also creates adorable scenes.

LAMB

With their sweet little *baas*, lambs bleat their way into the winner's circle. No one should feel *sheepish* when they ooh and aah with delight when looking at the large ears and gentle expression of this sweet-looking animal. Lambs are born with gangly legs, so newborns often seem to hop around fields full of excitement, adding to their colossal cuteness.

PIGLET

Get ready to go hog wild! With their fuzzy bodies and curly tails, newborn pigs are cute to the extreme. And students at Nottingham Trent University in the United Kingdom put that cuteness to good use: The stressed-out students have turned to piggy snuggles during exam time as a way to take a break, relax, and stay calm.

NATURALLY CUTE

Why We Find Baby Animals Adorable

Nothing makes you say *awww* like a fuzzy-eared kitten or a wiggly, chubby puppy. Baby animals are just plain cute—and there's even a scientific reason for it. Studies have shown that humans find baby animals (mammals specifically) to be adorable for the same reason they find baby humans to be adorable: They have big eyes, a small nose, a round face, and a small body.

This idea was first proposed in the 1940s by the Austrian zoologist Konrad Lorenz, who coined the term *Kindchenschema,* or "baby schema." That's the theory that baby animals evolved to be cute so that we're motivated to take care of them, protect them, and give them attention. These are all things that work in baby animals' favor and help them survive to adulthood.

Researchers in a 2018 study showed people various photos of puppies at different ages and then asked them to judge the pups' attractiveness. It turns out the dogs that were rated as most adorable were right around two months old, the same age that puppies are starting to fend for themselves, and about the time that humans come along to adopt them. Good timing!

KITTENS ARE PURR-FECTLY PRECIOUS

Kittens pour on the cute within days of being born. Though they are essentially blind and deaf during their first few weeks of life, kittens can communicate through purrs. They can feel the vibration of their mother's purr, a signal that says, "Come over here to stay warm and have something to eat"—two very important things for a newborn kitten! Kittens are also able to purr back to their mom to let her know they are safe. That communication technique is the cat's meow!

SPOTLIGHT

CUTEST ANIMAL FRIENDSHIPS

In the case of these adorable animal besties, opposites do attract.

PUPPY POWER
DOG AND PONY BECOME FAST FRIENDS

Spanky, a miniature horse, seemed to always be in a bad mood at his home in Washington State, U.S.A. That is, until a Jack Russell terrier puppy named Dally came into his life. One day when Spanky's humans, Francesca Carsen and Steve Rother, were training Spanky, Dally jumped from a stool right onto his back. Now these two friends have a lot of fun together. And that's no horsing around.

RESCUE REX
DOG SAVES BABY KANGAROO

One day when Rex, a wirehaired pointing griffon, was out walking in Victoria, Australia, with his human, Leonie Allan, he started acting strangely. Leonie soon realized Rex had noticed a baby kangaroo. It had been orphaned when its mother was hit by a car. Rex picked up the baby roo and placed it by Leonie's feet, nuzzling it and refusing to leave its side. Leonie brought the joey to a rescue-and-rehabilitation center, and when they visited a few weeks later, the little kangaroo immediately started playing with Rex. Friendship sealed!

ZOO PALS
GORILLA BONDS WITH RABBIT

Samantha, an older gorilla at a zoo in Pennsylvania, U.S.A., was lonely. Her companion had passed away, and zookeepers thought she could use a buddy. They carefully introduced a Dutch rabbit named Panda. Soon, Samantha was gently scratching Panda under the chin, patting her fur, and even sharing food with her new bunny pal.

FEARLESS FRIEND
GOOSE PROTECTS BULL

Right after Hamish, a Highland bull, was born on a farm in Waihirere, New Zealand, a furry friend in the form of a goose showed up and rested on his leg. Ever since that day, the two were pretty much inseparable. And if a cow or another bull got too close, the brave bird would screech, stretch out his neck, and chase the bulls away.

CURIOUS COMPANIONS
PUPPY KEEPS CHEETAH COMPANY

After he was born at a conservation center in Ohio, U.S.A., Emmett the cheetah cub required around-the-clock care. When he was transferred to the Columbus Zoo and Aquarium, zookeepers knew that the cautious cheetah needed a friend to help calm him. In bounded Cullen, a sweet puppy, to help comfort and soothe the cheetah. Soon Emmett was lonely no more.

BEASTY BESTIES
THE TORTOISE AND THE HIPPO

When Owen the hippo was a baby, a tsunami separated him from his family. Fortunately, he was rescued and taken to the Haller Park wildlife sanctuary in Kenya, Africa. When the other hippos wouldn't accept him, the park staff wanted to find him a companion, so they put him in the same enclosure as a 130-year-old giant tortoise named Mzee. Eventually, they became friends, napping and even swimming together. Sweet!

ROADSIDE PET ATTRACTION

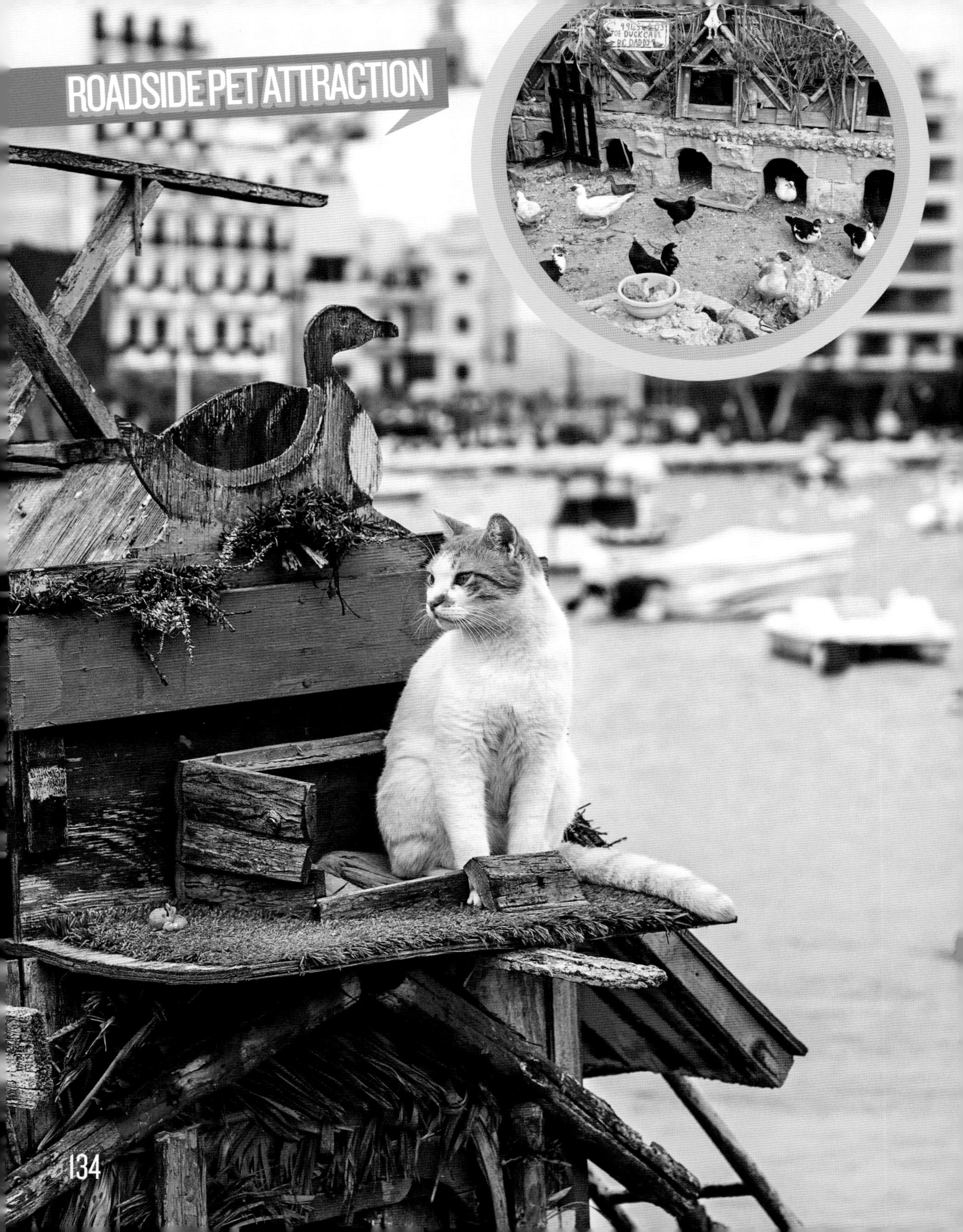

AN ISLAND WORTH FLOCKING TO

Welcome to a village where ducks rule!

On Malta's tiny Manoel Island in the Mediterranean, there's a seaside village where the feathered residents rule the roost. Duck's Village is home to ducks, chickens, and geese—not people—and t has plenty of amenities. Besides offering a beach and nearby swimming, the village has brightly colored homes made of wood, brick, stone, and recycled materials, which are crafted specifically to shelter the animals. Food and fresh water are brought in by local volunteer Joe Borg, who has taken on the task of keeping up the village for its residents. The village was initially inhabited by the birds, but since then stray cats, rabbits, and even guinea pigs have also moved in. Surprisingly, Duck's Village is peaceful. All the creatures that call it home find a way to get along, Borg says.

SUPER MAMA DUCK

There isn't a special village for ducks on Lake Bemidji in Minnesota, U.S.A., but there is one particular mama duck that could easily open a ducky daycare! In 2018, a female common merganser was seen swimming in the lake with 76 ducklings in tow. (Yes, 76!) Not all the youngsters were hers, however; this species of duck lays only about a dozen eggs at a time. Experts believe the superabundant ducklings may have split off from their parents and formed a larger group, which is then typically watched over by a few adults. Even though this group of 76 ducklings is much larger than average, observers said the mama duck kept things under control. Looks like she doesn't *quack* under pressure!

These pint-size pets are pros at protecting themselves.

ADORABLE, POKEY HEDGEHOGS

It's hard not to swoon over a pointy-nosed, palm-size pet described as a "pincushion with legs." Hedgehogs are simply precious. But that doesn't mean they don't have a prickly side—physically *and* in terms of personality.

European hedgehogs—like the fictional Mrs. Tiggy-winkle from the Beatrix Potter tale—roam wild in gardens (and hedges)! But the ones raised as pets are generally African pygmy hedgehogs, which are about seven inches (18 cm) long and covered in the trademark spines they use to protect themselves against predators.

Don't let their pudgy physique fool you: Hedgehogs are no slouches. In the wild, they run several miles at night looking for bugs and plants to eat. This means that when they're kept as pets, they need space—and possibly an exercise wheel—to get their wiggles out. But hedgehogs start to get active about the same time that you start to wind down for the day. Hedgehogs are nocturnal, which means their day starts around your dinnertime, and then they keep busy all night long! They also are most comfortable at warm temperatures and require a heat lamp to stay cozy. Needless to say, a critter scurrying around its enclosure with the light on doesn't make the best roommate. Many people keep their hedgies, as they're sometimes called, in a room other than their bedroom.

EVEN THOUGH THEY BOTH SPORT SPINY BODIES, HEDGEHOGS AND PORCUPINES ARE UNRELATED.

Before you consider a pet hedgehog, check local and state rules about keeping one. Some places do not allow hedgehogs to be kept as pets.

WHY SO PRICKLY?

Those spines on the back of a hedgehog—each has between 3,000 and 5,000 of them—are made from the same stuff as your fingernails: keratin. Even though hedgehogs look a little bit like mini-porcupines, the two aren't related. In fact, hedgehogs' closest relatives are shrews and moles. The spines are a hedgehog's ultimate survival mechanism in the wild. When it is in danger, a hedgehog's spines stand out and crisscross each other, making the animal as prickly as possible. It also tucks in its head and legs to roll itself into a ball to protect its soft belly.

BATTLE OF THE CUTEST

In these throwdowns, the champions are *aww*-dorable!

CUTEST COLLECTIVE NAME

Cats are cute, but what's even more adorable is a whole gang of cats, also known as a clowder. So what could be cuter than a clowder? A grumble! That's what you get when you put a group of pugs together. It's dogs for the win!

DOGS **vs.** CATS

WINNER

BUNNY **vs.** KITTY

CUTEST CUP

A little foam can go a long way when making adorable latte art. A kitty peeking out of a mug is precious, but the puffy ears on the bunny overtook this battle. That's a whole *latte* cute!

WINNER

RABBIT VS. GUINEA PIG

TIE

CUTEST NOISE

Rabbits and guinea pigs have a lot in common: Both are furry and have whiskers, and both eat veggies. They also have the same way of showing they're content. If rabbits and guinea pigs are happy and they know it, they purr! Guinea pigs make their purr in their throat, while rabbits make theirs by rubbing their teeth together. This one is a *purr*-fect tie.

AKITA VS. POTBELLIED PIG

CURLIEST TAIL

Nothing says Akita like the pup's signature tail, which curls up and over its back. And each Akita holds its tail in a slightly different position. But is it curlier than a pig's tail? You might not think so, but if it's a potbellied pig, Akitas have the win. Potbellies have perfectly straight tails. Only a domestic farm pig—with its typically curlicue tail—can compete with an Akita.

WINNER

Check out some of the many sweet, weird, and wonderful presidential pets that have called the White House home!

CUTE (AND COOL!) PRESIDENTIAL PETS

Nearly every U.S. president has had a pet that roamed the halls (and gardens) of the White House while in office, but President John F. Kennedy had the most pet-friendly White House of all. The 35th president practically had a small zoo! From parakeets and hamsters all the way up to ponies, the president, First Lady Jacqueline Kennedy, and their young children,

Caroline and John Jr., hosted a menagerie of pets at 1600 Pennsylvania Avenue.

There were a handful of dogs, including an Irish wolfhound, an Irish cocker spaniel, a German shepherd, a Welsh terrier, a French poodle, and Pushinka, the daughter of Strelka, the first dog in space. (Pushinka was a gift from the leader of the Soviet Union at the time, Nikita Khrushchev.) The Kennedys also had a

cat named Tom Kitten, a canary named Robin, parakeets named Bluebell and Maybelle, hamsters named Debbie and Billie, and a rabbit named Zsa Zsa. The people of Ireland gave John Jr. a pony named Leprechaun. Tex, a brown pony, and Macaroni, a part-Shetland pony, were both gifts to Caroline, who sometimes rode them on the White House lawn. Hail to the pets in chief!

PRESIDENT GEORGE WASHINGTON (1789–1797)
Washington kept horses and hounds, and his wife, Martha, had a parrot.

PRESIDENT ABRAHAM LINCOLN (1861–1865)
Lincoln had dogs, cats, rabbits, goats, and a turkey.

1800s

PRESIDENT JAMES BUCHANAN (1857–1861)
Buchanan kept dogs and a pair of bald eagles.

PRESIDENT BENJAMIN HARRISON (1889–1893)
Harrison had dogs and two pet opossums named Mr. Reciprocity and Mr. Protection.

PRESIDENT LYNDON JOHNSON WOULD "SING" WITH HIS DOG YUKI.

PRESIDENT JOHN F. KENNEDY'S DOGS, CHARLIE AND PUSHINKA, IN FRONT OF THE WHITE HOUSE

PRESIDENT THEODORE ROOSEVELT (1901–1909)
Roosevelt kept many dogs, a snake, a hyacinth macaw, two cats, kangaroo rats, a flying squirrel, guinea pigs, parrots, chickens, and many wild animals.

PRESIDENT CALVIN COOLIDGE (1929–1933)
Coolidge had many dogs, birds, and cats, plus a donkey and two raccoons.

1900s

PRESIDENT HERBERT HOOVER (1923–1929)
Hoover had many dogs—from shepherds to terriers—and a pair of alligators.

PRESIDENT JOHN F. KENNEDY (1961–1963)
Kennedy had many dogs, plus a cat, hamsters, a rabbit, and birds.

INDIAN DOMINO COCKROACH

CUTE-AT-A-GLANCE

142

PIGS

1 CUTEST FUNDRAISER

Pucker up for a good cause: A popular fundraiser, especially for pet-rescue organizations, is a dog kissing booth! Pups sit inside a box with a cut out window and give a lick to anyone who wants to *paws* and make a donation.

2 CUTEST CUDDLERS

A mother pig sticks close to her piglets until they are grown. When they sleep, the piglets snuggle in a pile and seem to prefer to sleep nose-to-nose! Squeal!

3 CUTEST SPOTS

Many people think of cockroaches as pests that they want *out* of their house. But some cockroaches actually make good pets—and are even polka-dotty cute. The Indian domino cockroach looks exactly like what its name implies: a domino tile! Its white spots appear as if they were dabbed on with a paintbrush.

CAT BACKPACK

4 CUTEST COUPLE

There's more to love about lovebirds than their affectionate name. Lovebirds stay together as a couple for life. Sometimes when they have been apart or have had a stressful episode, they feed each other when they reunite afterward. Talk about a perfect pair!

5 CUTEST ACCESSORY

Here's a way to make your chicken stand out in the flock: Give her a little bling! You can buy charm anklets for chickens in a variety of colors, with dangly hearts, flowers, and even peace signs. Someone is ready to strut around the farm!

6 CUTEST FORM OF TRAVEL

Have cat, will travel. This backpack is for those pet owners who simply can't be apart from their kitty. You can take your cat for a stroll while the air holes keep it safe—and the semi-sphere window provides a space-age-style view!

LOVEBIRDS

CHICKEN CHARM ANKLET

VIRTUAL PETS!

Cute "care-bots" bring real comfort.

As you get ready to feed your pet harp seal some fish for dinner—wait! You can't have a baby harp seal as a pet! But you can if the harp seal is actually a "care-bot."

PARO, a "personal therapeutic robot," was invented by Takanori Shibata, a scientist at Japan's National Institute of Advanced Industrial Science and Technology. First introduced in 2003, the special care-bot looks like an adorable harp seal, with fluffy white fur and large black eyes. But this seal doesn't need fish to eat. Instead, PARO is charged when it "sucks" on an electric pacifier.

What makes PARO so special? Humans are wired to connect to other people—and to pets. But when some people age, they may start to experience symptoms of dementia (a decline in memory or other thinking skills). That may mean they are unable to care for a living pet, since they might forget to feed their animal or get confused about its needs. That's when the simulated seal can make a big difference: PARO was designed to comfort and soothe patients with dementia. Cuddling with a pet, even if that pet is a care-bot, can help calm them down when they feel agitated, providing a tremendous emotional benefit. And PARO—which is loaded with sensors to detect touch, sound, light, heat, and movement—can actually respond to affection: When patients stroke PARO's fur, the seal responds as if it were alive. It moves its head and legs and makes sounds. PARO even imitates the voice of a real baby harp seal!

TAKANORI SHIBATA AND PARO

EACH PARO
CAN LEARN TO
**RECOGNIZE
ITS OWN
NAME.**

**PARO IS ABOUT THE SAME
SIZE AS A LARGE CAT.**

CUTEST 145

You know your pet is adorable, but it's not always easy to show to the rest of the world.

HOW TO TAKE AWW-SOME PHOTOS OF YOUR PETS

We've all been there: As soon as you pull out a camera, your pet starts to wiggle, look away, and quickly lose patience. Here are some tips to capture your pet's cute side.

1

GET DOWN TO YOUR PET'S LEVEL.
Taking a photo at eye level gives a personal, authentic look.

2

MAKE SOME NOISE.
Perked-up ears and a curious expression majorly up the cute factor. When you and your pet are in position, make a kissy noise or call your pet's name. This only works once or twice before you start causing confusion, so have your camera ready!

3

TRY AN ALTERNATIVE ANGLE.
A sitting pup makes for a classic portrait, but also consider mixing it up. Focus on your dog's wet nose, or cross his paws while he is asleep by the fire. Think about your pet's best feature and zoom in!

Remember that patience is key! If your pet gets bored with a photo shoot, call it quits and try again later. There will always be another opportunity to capture a cute pet pic.

4

TAKE AN ACTION SHOT.
If your pet is an extreme wiggler, embrace it! Catch your bunny in mid-leap as she bounds through the grass or your dog splashing into a lake to fetch a ball. If you're making a video, try the slow-motion or time-lapse option to add some drama (or humor!) to your pet's playtime.

5

PLAY WITH FILTERS.
Animals with dark fur can be tricky to photograph. Catch your black kitty in a sunspot to shed some natural light on the subject. Or, after you've taken the photo, experiment with your camera's filters to help bring out kitty's features.

CHAPTER 6

PETS THAT RUN, HOP, FLY, AND SLITHER—THESE ATHLETIC OVERACHIEVERS CAN BE HARD TO KEEP UP WITH!

Are you up for spending time with some of the most energetic pets out there? These critters are among the fastest and most flexible furry (and scaly and feathered) friends in the world.

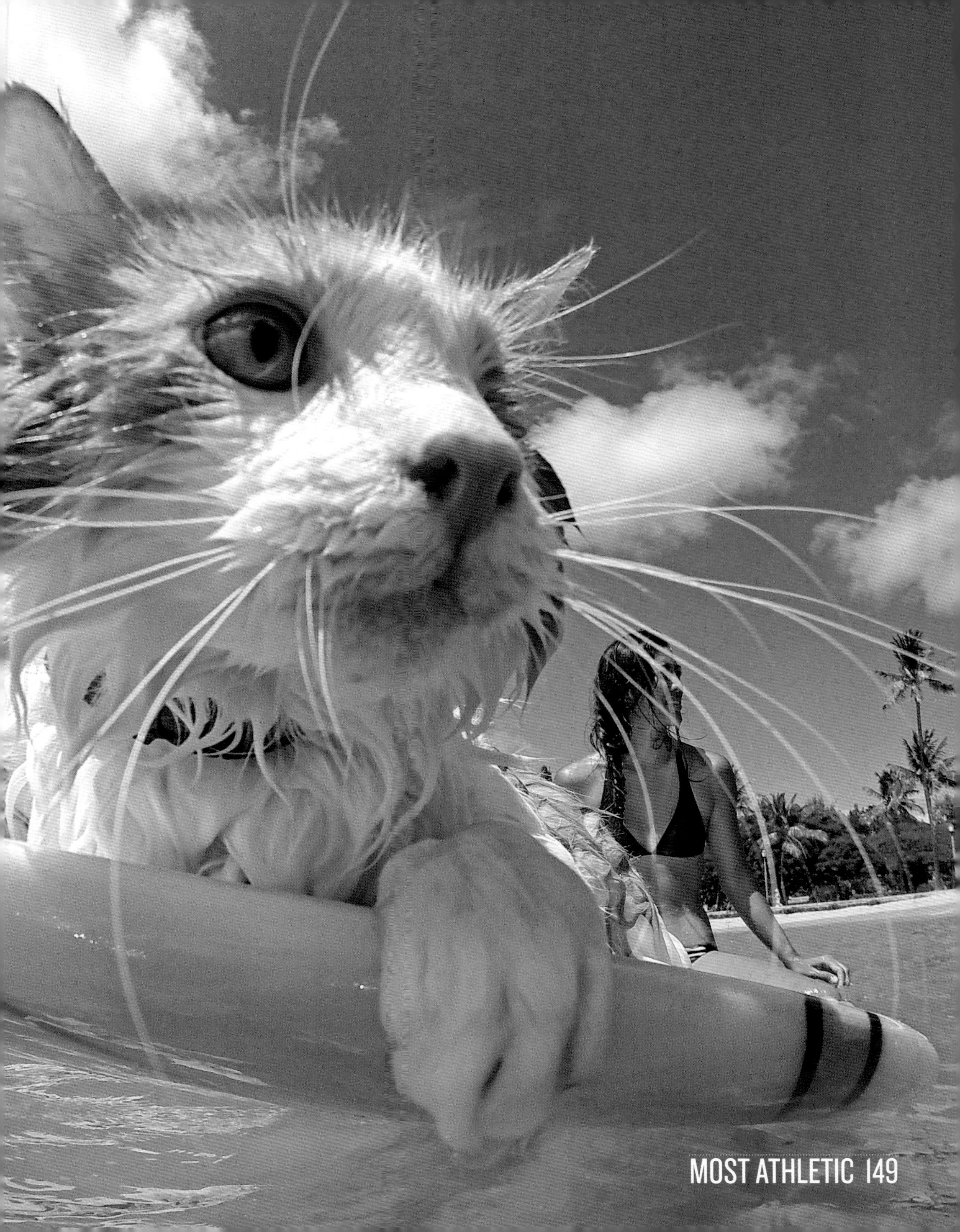

THE RABBIT

Run, rabbit, run! Bunnies boast blazing speed—in the wild, they can sprint at top speeds of 35 miles an hour (56 km/h), which they do to avoid becoming dinner for a weasel or a hawk. They also run in a zigzag pattern to avoid being caught. Because it's in their nature to be very active, rabbits kept as pets benefit from homemade backyard obstacle courses, which owners can make out of cardboard, plastic, wood, and hay. Agility courses allow pet rabbits to get the exercise they need to keep their muscles strong, stay a healthy weight, and have a hopping good time!

"BINKING"—JUMPING HIGH AND QUICKLY CHANGING DIRECTION— IS HOW A RABBIT SHOWS IT'S HAPPY OR EXCITED.

NUMBER OF BREEDS IN THE U.S.A.: **49**

LIFE SPAN: **7–10 YEARS**

WEIGHT: **2–20 POUNDS (1–9 KG)**

DIET: **GRASSES AND OTHER PLANTS**

NAME FOR BABIES: **KIT**

NAME FOR FEMALES: **DOE**

NAME FOR MALES: **BUCK**

AGE WHEN TEETH STOP GROWING: **NEVER**

THE RUNNERS-UP...

These pets really know where the action is.

HIGHEST **HIKER**

LLAMAS

This sure-footed South American pack animal can carry large loads weighing as much as 75 pounds (34 kg). Llamas were first domesticated by people living in the Andes thousands of years ago. They can travel for 20 miles (32 km) in a single day, and llamas' wide feet make them extremely stable hikers, which is important when navigating rocky terrain. A winner indeed!

FASTEST CANINE
GREYHOUND

These super sprinters can reach speeds of more than 40 miles an hour (64 km/h). Large lungs and a heart that can pump five times a second bring oxygen to the dog's muscles, powering them for short bursts. Even pharaohs in ancient Egypt used greyhounds to chase speedy desert animals, such as rodents. But don't expect greyhounds to keep up that activity level all the time: Their fondness for naps has earned them the nickname "the 40-mile-an-hour couch potato."

PREMIER PUSH-UP
LIZARD

These reptilian tough-guys love to flex their muscles. But scientists think that male lizards use the push-ups display to show off to other males—not to stay in shape. In the wild, they live in noisy forests, and because it's easy to see the push-ups, they use the visual display to warn rivals and mark their territory.

NIMBLEST KITTY
BENGAL CAT

This feline only looks wild! The Bengal is a descendant of the wild Asian leopard cat, but this athletic, muscular feline is indeed a house cat. Bengals possess a kitten-like energy into adulthood, and they love to climb and play fetch, making them our choice for most energetic cat.

Don't look away—these superactive pets might be gone in a flash.

BEST **REFLEXES**
PRAYING MANTISES

Praying mantises are some flexible pets! They can turn their heads 180 degrees—very cool—but they win this category for their lightning-fast reflexes. When eating, praying mantises snap up insects faster than a house fly moves away from a fly swatter. And young mantises can leap on prey faster than a blink of an eye.

CHAMPION **CHASERS**
BORDER COLLIES

These herding dogs were bred to run all day long, and it shows. A walk around the block will not cut it for them; these pets need a few hours of vigorous activity every day. When herding, these workaholics have many tricks: They crouch and creep and then flash forward in a burst of speed, all aimed at moving the sheep where they need to go.

MOST ATHLETIC JUMPERS

KILLIFISH

This colorful aquarium fish has been known to seek adventure—by jumping out of its tank! But the behavior is in its nature: In the wild, the freshwater fish live in small ponds that can dry up, so they jump from puddle to puddle seeking water. To keep track of this escape artist, it's best for owners to make sure the killie's environment is totally secure.

MIGHTIEST RACERS

MICE

Mice might be too busy to appreciate being named winners. They will run three miles (5 km) on an exercise wheel every night! Why do they do it? We're not sure, but scientists recently found that even wild mice choose to run on a wheel placed in their environment. And just like their housebound buddies, the wild mice ran in one- or two-minute sprints at a time.

A DOMESTIC CAT
CAN RUN AS FAST
AS **30 MILES
AN HOUR**
(48 KM/H) OVER
SHORT DISTANCES.

STRUCK BY ZOOMIES!

What's the opposite of a zombie? A zoomie!

It happens in cat households around the world: A kitty, curled up sound asleep, gets a twitch in her ear. She pops up, jumps down from her comfy chair, and then, out of nowhere, sprints around the house—this way and that—seemingly for absolutely no reason.

That cat has the zoomies—also known as frenetic random activity periods, or FRAPs. Why the need for speed? Experts say that indoor cats have a lot of pent-up energy that they need to release. In the wild, cats are hunting, stalking, and on high alert—all things that take energy. None of these things happen in the safety and comfort of a home, which also happens to have a continuously full bowl of kibble.

These energy releases are normal, but it can be a sign that your cat is looking for some stimulation. Make sure to play with your cat; toss toys or wave a play stick with a feather on the end. Cats of all ages need to get their wiggles out.

Also, be aware: Zoomies can be contagious! If you have more than one cat, one zoomie may set off a chain reaction.

YOUR OUTDOOR CAT MAY GET MORE EXERCISE THAN YOU THINK.

Ever wonder where your kitty goes when you open the door and he scurries outside? He may wander farther than you suspect! And he may get into some mischief along the way. A recent cat-tracking project fitted cats with GPS collars and then looked at where they went. Most of the cats stayed close to their homes, but some explored deeper into natural areas, like woods, and still others visited nearby houses looking for a snack!

A 2012 study revealed that cats do more than go for a romp when unattended: Free-range cats—including ones that are "feral," or don't have an owner, kill at least a billion birds every year in the United States. Cats have natural instincts to hunt, even when they aren't hungry. Here are some tips for protecting birds:
• Keep your cat indoors as much as possible.
• Take your cat for an outdoor walk on a harness if he'll tolerate it.
• Fit your cat with a special collar that warns birds that your cat is nearby. (These collars usually jingle, or they are brightly colored.)

SPORTY PETS

Whether on land, in the water, or in the air, these pets really bring their A game.

BALANCE BROTHERS
PADDLE-BOARDING GOATS

Two goat brothers, Apollo and Zeus, know just what to do when the stress of goat living gets to them. They take to a paddleboard and float along the waters near Jupiter, Florida, U.S.A. And if they want to mix it up, they might just decide to take out a kayak.

DARING DOGGIES
SNOWBOARDING BULLDOGS

Hitting the slopes came naturally for these bulldogs from Southern California, U.S.A. After mastering skateboarding, Tillman, Lyle, Rose, and Sully let the snow fly when they learned to shred the slopes.

SURFING SUPREME
WAVE-RIDING CAT

Nānākuli is a one-eyed rescue kitty who likes to hang ten. He takes to the waves in the Hawaiian Islands, U.S.A., where he learned to surf by tagging along with his humans until he mastered the art of going solo. Epic!

RIDING BUDDIES
PONY AND CORGI RODEO

A Missouri, U.S.A., farmer came home one night to an unexpected sight: Her miniature pony, Cricket, was being ridden by a neighbor's corgi! The persistent pup bounces up and down a few times before hopping onto his pal's back and taking a spin around the farm.

HALF-PIPE HEROES
SKATEBOARDING BUDGIES

Small pet birds such as budgies (also known as parakeets) can grasp small skateboards with their claws. And naturally, once they are on the board, they can ride the ramps or shred the half-pipe.

MONUMENTAL LEAPERS
SPLASH DOGS

These athletic dogs launch themselves off docks or platforms as they leap into the air to catch balls before a soft landing in water. The most athletic pups can jump more than 30 feet (9 m)—or as far as a three-story building is tall.

MOST ATHLETIC 159

CANIDAE

HOP OVER TO CALAVERAS COUNTY FOR FROG JUMPING.

More than 150 years ago, the American author Mark Twain wrote a fictional short story about a frog-jumping contest in Calaveras County, California, that later inspired locals to make one a reality.

Believe it or not, that competition is still hoppin'! Frog "jockeys"—competitors who bring their locally caught California bullfrogs to the annual event—are serious about jumping. Anyone can enter, and if you don't have a frog, you can borrow one from the "frog spa" on-site. Here's the way the competition works: Each frog is allowed three jumps in a row, and the straight-line distance from the starting spot to the last hop is measured for a final score. There are three days of jump-offs, and on the fourth day, the top 50 jumpers are entered into the finals. The reigning world record holder (since 1986) is Rosie the Ribiter, who scored 21 feet 5.75 inches (6.6 m).

There are strict rules about the care and humane treatment of the frogs. In fact, the best jumpers tend to be the ones that are handled the least. The frogs are also athletes in their own right and, like professional long jumpers, do best when their muscles are warm and limber. Contestants have found that frogs that are kept in a cool environment don't jump as far.

AMERICAN BULLFROGS: SUPER HOPPERS

American bullfrogs *(Rana catesbeiana)* are jumpy. The largest of all North American frogs, they can grow to eight inches (20 cm) or more and weigh up to one and a half pounds (0.7 kg). In the wild, bullfrogs' legs serve them well by being able to spring to attack birds, reptiles, fish, and insects. Only males make that deep bullfrog *moo*.

SOME FROGS CAN JUMP MORE THAN 20 TIMES THEIR OWN BODY LENGTH.

SWIMMING PIGS!

Pigs may not be able to fly, but they can certainly swim! And some are making a big splash with their skills.

Kama, a pig from Hawaii, U.S.A., started a family tradition of catching waves in 2014. This piggy stood on the front end of a surfboard while his human in the back did the steering. Then Kama's son, Kama 2, took to surfing—and then along came Kama 3, Kama 2's surfing daughter! Cowabunga? More like *Pig*abunga, dude!

But Hawaii isn't the only tropical paradise for pig water play. On one island in the Bahamas, pigs are the main attraction. No one knows how a group of semiferal pigs ended up on an uninhabited island called Big Major Cay. Some think they may have swum over from a nearby shipwreck; others say residents of neighboring islands dropped them off there. Regardless of how they made it to Big Major Cay, they are now local celebrities. Tourists take day trips to hang out with the pigs on the white-sand beach and even go for a swim with them in the ocean! When the pigs hear the boats approaching, they typically swim out to greet them. Between 30 and 40 pigs live on the island, and a volunteer group has formed to monitor the pigs' diet and health and to make sure they have freshwater to drink.

PIGS MAY BE ABLE TO **SURF**, BUT THEY CAN'T HANG 10! THEY HAVE **FOUR TOES ON EACH FOOT**, BUT ONLY TWO TOUCH THE GROUND.

MOST ATHLETIC 163

Who is going to muscle their way to the top?

AGILE ANIMALS

QUARTER HORSE vs. GREYHOUND

WINNER

QUICKEST SPRINTER

There's no doubt that greyhounds and quarter horses both have pickup, but when you clock their individual speeds, quarter horses win by a nose. At top speed, quarter horses can sprint 55 miles an hour (89 km/h), about as fast as a car on a highway. Greyhounds, the fastest dog, can reach speeds of 43 miles an hour (69 km/h).

TURTLE vs. TORTOISE

FASTEST SLOWPOKE

You've heard what happens when a tortoise races a hare, but what happens when it goes up against a turtle? It's a whole different ending. The world's fastest tortoise was clocked at .63 miles an hour (1 km/h), but soft-shelled turtles can go at least three times faster on land. And in the water, some turtles can swim more than 20 miles an hour (32 km/h)!

WINNER

BEST FETCHER

Golden retrievers and border collies are both enthusiastic fetchers, but which one is the MVP? Sorry, golden retriever, but you take the silver this time. A golden retriever named Augie was able to hold five tennis balls in his mouth, but Rose, a border collie and Labrador mix, caught seven Frisbees, thrown one at a time, and held them all in her mouth at once.

WINNER

BORDER COLLIE vs. RETRIEVER

NEWFOUNDLAND vs. BULLDOG

BEST SWIMMER

Sturdy bulldogs look like they're up for about any athletic competition—except if it involves swimming! The breed's big head and round torso don't help them in the floating department. Newfoundlands, however, were made for water sports. With partially webbed feet and a strong build, they're sometimes used as water rescue dogs.

WINNER

HIGHEST JUMPER

In a jumping contest, one of these leaps to the top of the podium: the chinchilla! Thanks to that long tail, which they use for balance, chinchillas are expert jumpers—able to leap as high as six feet (1.8 m)! Ferrets' strength is in their flexibility and ability to move side to side, not vertically. They can't jump higher than about two feet (0.6 m).

CHINCHILLA vs. FERRET

WINNER

THE IDITAROD

Every year, teams of dogs race from Anchorage to Nome, Alaska, U.S.A., in a taxing test of endurance.

FIRST RACE HELD:
March 3, 1973

LENGTH OF RACE:
1,000
miles
(1,600 km)

AVERAGE NUMBER OF DOGS ON A TEAM:
16

CHECKPOINTS ON SOUTHERN ROUTE:
24

DAYS TO COMPLETE:
8 or 9
for winning teams

CHECKPOINTS ON NORTHERN ROUTE:
23

FASTEST WINNING TIME:
8 days, **3** hours, **40** minutes, and **13** seconds

SLOWEST WINNING TIME:
20 days, **15** hours, **2** minutes, and **7** seconds

SECRET MESSENGERS TAKE FLIGHT.

Long before emails and texts, there was another way to communicate that was far more secretive and didn't involve a battery charger: pigeons! Sending a message via pigeon goes back at least 2,000 years, when Romans used them to communicate during battles. When World War I broke out, new technology like the telephone and telegraph wasn't reliable, and conversations could be spied on by the enemy. So homing pigeons were brought in to get the job done.

Homing pigeons instinctually know to return to their roost, but they're able to navigate in only one direction: home. So, they were carried with soldiers into the field and released with information of importance for military commanders, which would be delivered when the pigeons returned to their roost. Small capsules were attached to their legs. Sometimes, larger packages that included maps or photos were fastened to their backs. The pigeons could fly as far as 600 miles (965 km) back to their roost at speeds of about 40 miles an hour (64 km/h)—and they were reliable: They almost always reached their home, where they'd receive a treat on arrival. The pigeons were so efficient that they could be released from an aircraft, with a note from the pilot explaining what he was seeing on the battlefield from above, and the commanders on the ground would go to their roost to get a quick update.

THE U.S. MILITARY ENLISTED MORE THAN **200,000 PIGEONS** DURING WORLD WAR I AND WORLD WAR II TO **RELAY MESSAGES** AND CONDUCT SURVEILLANCE.

A PIGEON'S LIFE OFF THE BATTLEFIELD

Pigeons may be war heroes, but they are also everyday birds. It doesn't take long to find one in many city parks! Some people even keep domestic ones as pets. We know from their history that they are smart, and they are social. They prefer to be around other pigeons—or at least people who give them a lot of attention. A reminder: Pigeons should not be taken from the wild to be kept as pets. There are rescue organizations that adopt out pigeons that need homes.

ATHLETIC-AT-A-GLANCE

BINI THE BUNNY

RAT SNAKE

1 BEST SLAM DUNK

Bini the Bunny is a serious hoopster. The Holland lop has a world record for slam-dunking seven bunny-size basketballs on a bunny-size hoop in one minute. Bini's human noticed that Bini liked playing with a toy ball, so he got him a small hoop and basketball. Before long, and with some motivation from treats, Bini was a dunk master.

2 HARDEST-WORKING FISH

Here's a fish that is definitely a keeper: *Plecostomus*, also known as suckerfish, eat fish food that sinks to the bottom of a fish tank. They also suck up algae that accumulate on the tank's sides. Finishing leftovers and cleaning up his room? Give that fish a raise in his allowance!

3 FASTEST BITE

Snakes can literally strike as fast as a blink of the eye. But many people think only venomous snakes take quick bites. Not true: Researchers recently discovered that rat snakes, popular pets, strike their prey as fast, if not faster, than venomous snakes do. They need to lunge rapidly for the same reason as other snakes—to succeed at snatching lunch.

SUCKERFISH

GOAT YOGA

4 BEST RIGHT HOOK

You might want to avoid stepping into the ring with this pup! Boxers got their name because of their tendency to stand on their hind legs and box with their front paws. This usually happens when they are in a playful mood. What a knockout trick!

5 MOST ZEN WORKOUT

Don't be surprised if a goat jumps up on your back when you're in downward dog pose at one yoga studio in Oregon, U.S.A.! Customers at Goat Yoga do traditional yoga moves, but they do them outside and among a handful of goats that might walk between their legs, lie down next to them, and even burp in their ear!

6 MOST EFFICIENT BATHER

Dogs are Olympians at drying off after a bath. The moment after the water is turned off and they do that big shake, 70 percent of the water is off their body. Dogs have loose skin that can twist farther and faster than their backbones, generating enough force to get rid of most of the water on their body within four seconds.

BOXERS

DOG

DOGS AT WORK

THE **SUPER** SCENT-DETECTING **ABILITIES** OF HERDING AND HUNTING BREEDS MEAN THEY ARE OFTEN SELECTED TO TRAIN AS **SEARCH AND RESCUE DOGS.**

Humans and dogs have lived together for thousands of years, from the first time wolves started hanging around humans. Since then, we have gained from their amazing talents—and we've come to rely on them for all kinds of reasons. Dogs are loyal and extremely hardworking. Their sense of smell is estimated to be 10,000 times better than ours. And dogs love being challenged and will work tirelessly on a task.

The U.S. Department of Agriculture works with highly trained beagles, the "beagle brigade," at airports and ports of entry. They sniff out agricultural products and plants that carry diseases or invasive species before they enter the United States. These beagles can search a piece of luggage in mere seconds, when it would take a human much longer.

Arson dogs put their noses to a different test: They help fire investigators determine whether a fire was an accident or set by someone on purpose. These working dogs give their handlers a signal when they smell fire accelerants, and they can search through a fire scene in 30 minutes, a job that could take humans days.

Hardworking search and rescue dogs use their fine-tuned instincts to find victims of earthquakes buried in rubble or skiers trapped by an avalanche. They can also sniff out the scent of a person who has gone missing, both in the wilderness and in the water.

Regardless of where they are called to work, these fantastic fidos have earned their place as our best friends.

BACKYARD DOG-AGILITY COURSE

Want to help your dog get her wiggles out and teach her some new tricks along the way? Why not make an agility course in your backyard? There's no need to go out and buy new things; you probably already have most of these supplies. It turns out that dogs like to play with the same stuff as you.

1

TUNNEL RUN

Those flexible tunnels that you crawled through during your toddler years are perfect tunnel runs for pups! Training tip: At first, a tunnel may seem scary to your dog. Show her how it's done the first time and encourage her to follow you. Next, have her sit and wait at one end, and then call to her to come from the other end. Give her a treat as soon as she's made it through.

2

CONE WEAVING

Pull out those mini orange cones you use for soccer, and voilà! You have the perfect tool to set up a weaving course for your dog. To teach your dog how to weave in and out of cones, start by walking her through on a leash, offering a treat after she finishes a line of cones. Next, do the same weaving pattern off-leash, but have her follow you while you hold out a treat in your hand. Before long, she'll be an expert weaver all on her own!

Remember: Never force your dog to do something she doesn't want to do. If she's resistant, wait and try again another time. Also, make sure you only offer positive encouragement. This should be all about fun for your pup!

TIP: If you don't have a Hula-Hoop, a pool noodle also works well as a jump.

3

HULA-HOOP JUMPING

Your pooch will be ready for the circus after this trick. Ask a parent or sibling to hold a Hula-Hoop vertically, with the bottom of the hoop touching the ground. As you did for the tunnel run trick, ask her to sit on one side of the hoop while you call her to come from the other side. Give her a treat. Slowly increase the height a few inches after she's successfully jumped through the hoop. Before long, she'll be ready for the big top! Again, if she's nervous, keep the hoop low.

CHAPTER 7

IT'S TIME TO SHINE A SPOTLIGHT ON SOME POPULAR PETS.

From fluff balls to scaly wonders, these pets come in all shapes and sizes. But they all have one thing in common—unique traits make them crowd-pleasers.

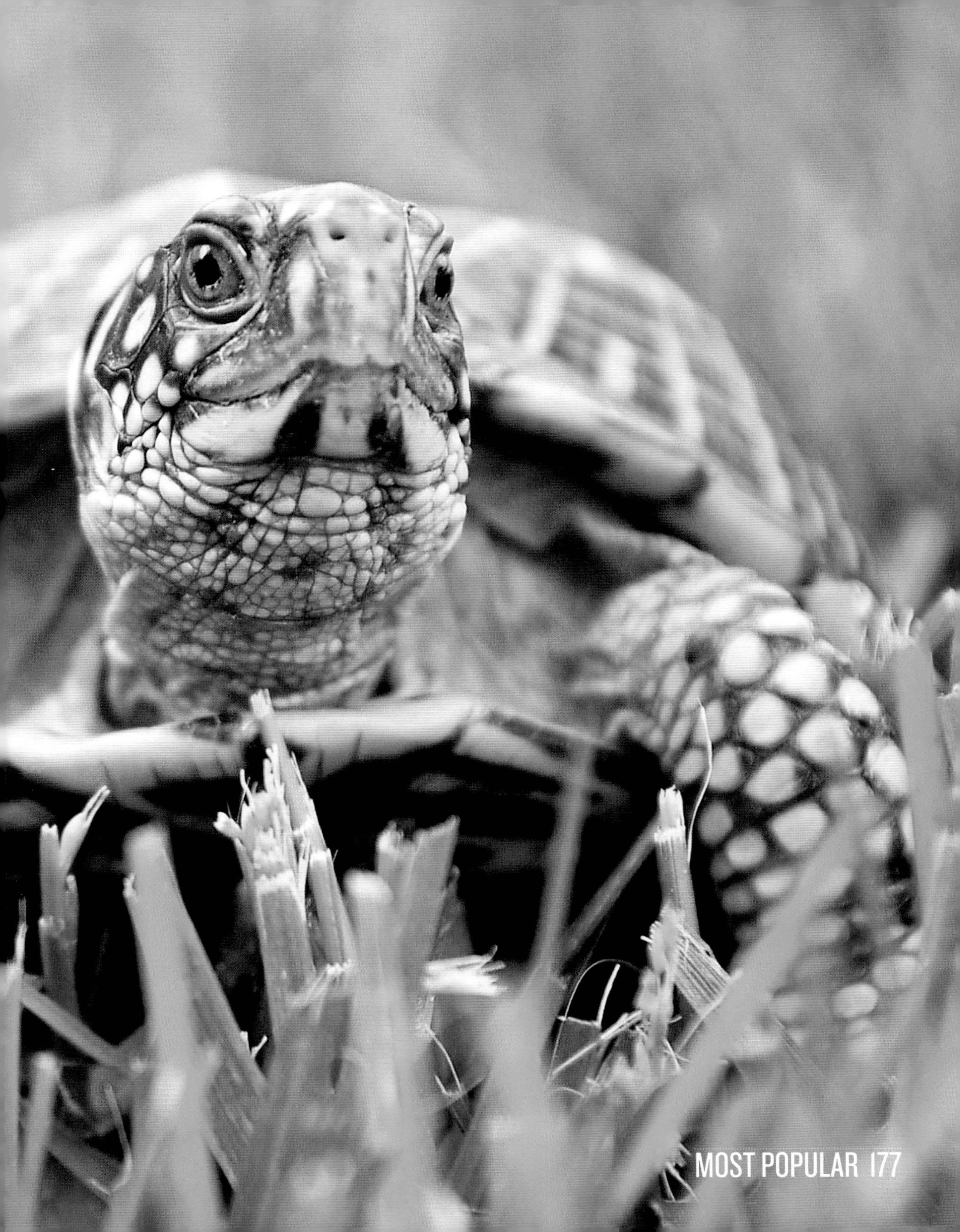

PERCENTAGE OF U.S. HOUSEHOLDS WITH FRESHWATER FISH: **10**

AVERAGE NUMBER OF FRESHWATER FISH IN A HOUSEHOLD: **11**

LIFE SPAN OF GOLDFISH: **UP TO 30 YEARS IN THE WILD**

LIFE SPAN OF BETTA FISH: **2–3 YEARS**

LENGTH OF GOLDFISH (IN THE WILD): **14 INCHES (36 CM)**

LENGTH OF BETTA FISH: **3 INCHES (7.6 CM)**

FRESHWATER FISH

I f you think there might be something fishy about this winner, you'd be right! When it comes to the sheer number of individual pets, freshwater fish (including favorites such as goldfish, betta fish, and zebrafish) are more popular than dogs or cats or horses or rabbits. An estimated 139 million freshwater fish splash around in home ponds and aquariums across the United States.

Fish are great pets for first-time pet owners and experienced aquarium enthusiasts alike, who often keep a number of these finned swimmers in one tank. But fish are awesome for reasons beyond their cool colors and mesmerizing motion: Studies have shown that watching fish swim can help reduce blood pressure and heart rate and put people in a happier mood. Now that's *fin*-tastic!

BETTA FISH HAVE THE ABILITY TO **BREATHE OXYGEN** ABOVE THE WATER'S SURFACE, USING AN ORGAN CALLED THE **LABYRINTH.**

These sought-after record holders have a lock on the top of the popular list.

MOST POPULAR **DOG BREED**

LABRADOR RETRIEVER

Move over, Rover. The Labrador is in the house! The Labrador has been in the number one spot on the American Kennel Club's list of popular dog breeds every year for nearly three decades. These sweet pups are not just popular—they are also friendly and super social. The breed's easygoing temperament also vaults it to the top of the list as rescue or guide dogs.

MOST POPULAR CAT COAT
TABBY

This winner is always dressed to impress. That's because the tabby cat is tops for its popular coat, with its swirls, blobs, and stripes. But tabbies are not one specific breed. Instead, the tabby's distinctive markings can be found in breeds like the American curl and the Scottish fold. Their most inspired marking may be the M shape that shows up on their forehead.

MOST POPULAR SNAKE
GARTER SNAKE

For beginning snake enthusiasts, the garter snake is a top choice. The slithering reptile is calm and pretty easy to care for. Usually reaching around three feet (0.9 m) long, they have great eyesight, love to climb, and are active during the day. Garters are harmless, but they can emit a foul smell when handled or upset.

Never take a box turtle or garter snake from the wild.

MOST POPULAR TURTLE
BOX TURTLE

Box turtles can live for decades, which means your box turtle could easily be around when you are in college. These popular orange-splotched reptiles get their name from how they can shut their shells and seal themselves inside an impenetrable "box." Box turtles thrive when they live outside in a protected shelter where they can be kept warm and that has hiding spots, such as hollow logs and brush.

MORE RUNNERS-UP ... Check out these popular but unusual companions.

MOST POPULAR **INSECT**

CRICKET

This is the only champ to sing itself into a top spot. In China, the tradition of keeping pet crickets dates back thousands of years. The insect's musical chirps make beautiful songs, and the popular pets are thought to bring good luck. Since cricket songs are rarely heard outdoors during the winter, they can be placed bedside in small cages for nighttime serenades when the weather turns cold.

MOST POPULAR **UP-AND-COMING PET**

CHICKEN

This is one *egg*-citing trend. While not many families own pet chickens, the number who do increased by 23 percent between 2013 and 2018! These friendly fowl aren't legal in every backyard. But in U.S. cities like Los Angeles and Chicago, keeping chickens allows families a way to have pets that give back—with some love and some eggs, that is.

MOST POPULAR
SALAMANDER

AXOLOTL

In Japan, axolotls (pronounced ACK-suh-LAH-tuhl) are perfectly popular aquatic pets. Their wide-set eyes, mouth, and whiskers give them an adorably sweet grin. This unique salamander lives in water and is also called the Mexican walking fish. In Mexico, where the amphibian originated, axolotls were revered by the ancient Aztecs. Today they are nearly extinct in the wild.

MOST POPULAR PONY

SHETLAND PONY

This is no one-trick pony. There are more Shetland ponies on Foula Island, off Scotland's northeast coast, than people! Which makes sense, because the popular pony was first bred on the Shetland Islands more than 2,000 years ago. But the breed hasn't remained on the islands, and even celebrities such as Hilary Duff and Brad Pitt have owned a Shetland. As a young girl, Queen Elizabeth II of the United Kingdom had a Shetland pony.

MOST POPULAR

Pooches strut their stuff at this Halloween costume party.

DOG PARADE

Yes, a dog dressed as a pumpkin is hilarious, but try this costume on for size: Four French bulldogs (aka Frenchies) dressed as French tourists sitting inside a homemade pup-size New York sightseeing bus. These are the kind of next-level costumes that can be seen every year at the Tompkins Square Halloween Dog

Parade in New York City. Dubbed the "largest dog costume parade in the world," the event draws about 500 dogs and upwards of 25,000 people who come to see the pooches strut their stuff in the city's East Village.

Anyone can join the parade, but creative costumes are what this long-standing tradition is all about—like a dog popping out of his

THE TOUR DE CORGI

While the Tompkins Square parade is come one, come all, an annual parade in Fort Collins, Colorado, U.S.A., is on a smaller scale—or rather, a shorter-legged scale. The Tour de Corgi is a costume parade in which corgis can strut (or waddle) their stuff. Hundreds of corgis gather for a costume contest—with categories that include "Cutest Couple," "Like Human, Like Corgi," and "Baddest to the Bone." Recent costumed corgis included fairy princesses, bumblebees, and a spectacled Harry Potter riding in a Hogwarts Express dog stroller.

own selfie on a smartphone or a Pomeranian done up as King Tut.

And even though the dogs take center stage, their owners often get in on the action, too—with human-pet pairings such as matching unicorn outfits, an Ewok pup and a Princess Leia handler, and even a pup dressed as a hot dog and its owner dressed up as a hot dog vendor.

MVPs: MOST VALUABLE PET TRENDS

Everywhere you look, pets are becoming trendy social media stars or getting pampered by their people with the latest treats. Here are a few standout crowd-pleasers.

TOP TOPPERS
SNAKES IN HATS

This trend is truly over-the-top! Snake owners place tiny hats—including fedoras, bowlers, sombreros, and baseball caps—on their reptiles' heads and post the pics online. This 10-gallon trend went viral, and more than 21,000 people joined an online community to share fun pictures.

FAST-FOOD FOODIES
PET MENUS

From "puppuccino" (whipped cream in a cup) to good-dog specials (an unseasoned hamburger), dining out has really gone to the dogs! Some fashionable fast-food chains offer special menus just for pets. So if your pooch has a hankering for a dog biscuit with peanut butter and vanilla or a vanilla soft serve with a miniature bone on top, throw him the keys and send him to a drive-through window. Just kidding! Ask an adult to drive.

JINGLE BELLS
SANTA PHOTOS

Pet stores, rescue shelters, and adoption organizations all hold events around the holidays where families can take pics as Santa sits with their calico cat or their dashing Doberman—or even their ho-ho hamster! In many cases, the small cost for the photo raises money to benefit local shelters and help pets in need all year-round.

PINT-SIZE PICASSO
PAINTING POOCH

When Dee Dee Murry first gave her dachshund, Hallie, a paintbrush, it was a whimsical idea to brighten up a humdrum day. After Hallie suddenly went blind a few months later, Dee Dee was surprised that the pint-size Picasso continued her painting! A local paper covered the story, it went viral, and Dee Dee decided to sell the paintings to support a local dog rescue organization. Nice!

HASHTAG HAPPENINGS
SOCIAL MEDIA STARS

You know your pet is fabulous. But how do you spread the word to the rest of the world? Hashtag it! Families and fans use social media and tags such as #Caturday on Saturday and #MeowMonday on Monday to showcase the *purr*-sonality of their cats on a certain day of the week. Trendy hashtags such as #TongueOutTuesday and #WaterDogWednesday allow people to look at adorable photos all in one place.

MOST POPULAR 187

WHO'S THE GOOD DOG?

This food truck is for the dogs.

Now this is a truck that any dog would want to chase after. Fetch is a restaurant on wheels in the Birmingham, Alabama, U.S.A., area that caters only to pups. And its menu will even have the humans' mouths watering!

One of the more *pup*-ular items at Fetch is the ice cream, and the flavors cater to a dog's palate: maple bacon and peanut butter. If your pup prefers her ice cream on a stick, you can order up a chicken Popsicle, which is made with yogurt and chicken broth and served on a rawhide stick! (You can also order a peanut butter version.) The doggy ice-cream treats are made lactose-free. (Lactose isn't good for dogs' bellies.)

But there's more to this food truck than ice cream. Other desserts and treats include "bacon cheezits," biscuits made with—you guessed it!—cheese and bacon, along with specially decorated organic cookies.

The Fetch truck makes the rounds at community and kid-friendly events, and of course, dog parks.

188

"PUPCAKE" PARADISE

Dogs in Beverly Hills, California, U.S.A., should expect nothing less than glamorous treats. Your prince or princess is covered at Sprinkles, the world's first cupcake bakery, located in the heart of the city's famous shopping area. Its "pup-cakes" are sugar-free and can come with a yogurt frosting.

THE MOST POPULAR LIZARD IS... A DRAGON?

Bearded dragons don't exactly have beards, and they definitely aren't dragons. But they are a popular reptile pet known for their easygoing, social vibe. "Beardies," as they're sometimes called, hail from the land down under: Australia. That beard is actually a bunch of spines that normally lie flat. When the lizard feels threatened, its throat expands, and those spines stand up, making the beardie look larger and extra fierce. But don't worry: In the comforts of home, without the threats of the wild, pet bearded dragons rarely show this behavior.

One behavior that is more likely to be seen is a friendlier one—in the form of a wave. Yup, from time to time, females (and once in a while, males) lift a front leg in the air and give a wave. This is a submissive gesture, usually meaning that they come in peace and don't mean any harm.

Beardies do have some specific needs, and keeping toasty warm is one of them. Outdoors, in the wilds of Australia, bearded dragons get lots of sunlight. Indoors, the light has to be supplied in the form of a special lamp designed for reptiles that emits UVA and UVB radiation—two types of ultraviolet light. These heat lamps help ensure the "basking" end of their enclosure stays around 100°F (38°C) during the day.

HOW TO BATHE YOUR DRAGON

Keeping a bearded dragon hydrated and bathed can be a bit like creating a spa experience. The best way to make sure your bearded dragon is getting the right amount to drink is to use a spray bottle. After owners lightly mist them and their enclosure, bearded dragons will lick the droplets. They also like having a large dish of lukewarm water to soak in. Calming music and sliced cucumbers are optional!

FAVORITE MATCHUPS!

SOLO VS. WITH THEIR HUMAN

MOST POPULAR SLEEP SPOT

It turns out that dogs spend a lot of their time in the dog-house. Or at least in their own bed. A recent survey of dog owners revealed that 45 percent shared a sleeping space with their pup. But the majority of canine companions slept in a crate, in their own bed, or in various spots around the house, saving cuddle time with their humans for the daylight hours.

WINNER

CANNOLI VS. WHOOPIE PIE

MOST POPULAR TREAT

These dog treats look so good that you may wish you could sneak a bite! The Whippet Whoopie Pie from Le Marcel Bakery for Dogs in San Francisco, California, is made with dark carob cake and vanilla frosting. And the Collie Cannoli from Three Dog Bakery in Kansas City, Missouri, U.S.A., is made from a wheat-flour pizzelle cookie and dog-friendly ice cream. When it comes to dessert, there are no losers. It's a tie!

TIE

NATIONAL CAT DAY vs. NATIONAL DOG DAY

TIE

MOST POPULAR NATIONAL PET DAY

No need to fight like cats and dogs over this smackdown. National Dog Day, celebrated on August 26, recognizes the number of dogs that need to be rescued each year. Similarly, National Cat Day, celebrated on October 29, sets out to raise awareness about homeless cats. Sounds like both days are winners!

MOST POPULAR HOLIDAY TO BUY YOUR DOG A GIFT

Every day is a good day to spoil your pet, but a 2016 survey of dog owners found that certain holidays are more popular than others when it comes to giving their pets presents. No lumps of coal here: 48 percent of those surveyed gave their dogs a Christmas present. A dog's birthday was the second most popular, with 28 percent of pets enjoying a gift to "unwrap" on their birthday.

BIRTHDAY vs. CHRISTMAS

WINNER

UGA THE ENGLISH BULLDOG vs. JONATHAN THE HUSKY

WINNER

MOST POPULAR MASCOT

Jonathan was the University of Connecticut's mascot starting in 1933; since then, 14 other Jonathans have served in the role. Jonathan even has his own bobblehead! There have been 10 Ugas, the mascot of the University of Georgia (another U.S. school) since 1956. Uga is so popular that he can retreat to an air-conditioned doghouse next to the cheerleaders' platform during football games. That's a touchdown win for Uga!

THE MOST POPULAR PETS
IN THE U.S.

Pets, pets everywhere! Here are the total number of pets owned in the United States, by type of animal.

CATS:
94.2 million

FRESHWATER FISH:
139.3 million

DOGS:
89.7 million

BIRDS: 20.3 million

SALTWATER FISH: 18.8 million

SMALL ANIMALS: 14 million

REPTILES: 9.4 million

HORSES: 7.6 million

THIS 18TH-CENTURY PET WAS PRETTY SQUIRRELY.

Imagine if instead of a dog sitting near your desk watching you do homework, it was a squirrel. A real, bushy-tailed squirrel that you walked on a little leash and hand fed from a little dish of nuts you kept handy. Sound like a bizarre alternate universe or a fairy tale? This was real-life in the United States during the 18th and 19th centuries!

Sometimes taken from the wild and brought into people's homes and other times bought from a pet store, squirrels were once popular pets in the United States. Gray squirrels, red squirrels, and flying squirrels were all brought indoors and kept as companions, especially by wealthy families. Why the attraction? Squirrels were considered exotic compared with ordinary household pets—and it was fun to watch them race around and reward them with their favorite treat—nuts, of course! But there's a reason squirrels aren't popular today: They are wild animals with sharp claws. They need lots of space to run around—larger than the confines of a house. And they can be mischievous and destroy furniture and belongings. Squirrels are also territorial, so they can be aggressive.

By the 20th century, an overpopulation of squirrels in urban parks had given squirrels the reputation of being a menace, and they were no longer the sought-after pets that they once were. Today, many state and local governments don't allow people to keep squirrels as pets.

THAT'S NUTS! THIS SQUIRREL WAS A WHITE HOUSE VIP

The pet-squirrel fad had faded by the 1920s, when President Warren G. Harding was in office, but that didn't stop him from forming a bond with one that he called Pete. Pete hung around the White House grounds and became so comfortable with people that he would eat out of their hands. He sometimes ran through the White House halls and even turned up at important meetings!

A SQUIRREL'S TEETH NEVER STOP GROW-ING.

POPULAR-AT-A-GLANCE

SWEEPEE RAMBO

CHIA PET

1 MOST POPULAR UGLY DOG

Even though SweePee Rambo, a 17-year-old Chinese crested Chihuahua, was given the not-so-flattering title of World's Ugliest Dog at a Northern California ugly-dog contest in 2016, she still stole hearts. SweePee Rambo won the judges over with her batlike ears, tuft of white fur on her head, and tongue that stuck out one side of her mouth.

2 MOST POPULAR CAT NAME

Drumroll! According to an analysis by a pet insurance company, the most popular name for a female cat is Bella and for a male cat is Oliver. And it seems that humans' taste in cat names doesn't veer much from their favorite baby names: Over the past decade, Oliver ranked 38th on the list of most popular baby names for boys and Isabella (the formal version of Bella) ranked fourth for girls!

3 MOST POPULAR DESKTOP PET

If you think your dog has an unruly coat, check out this "pet." Chia pets, which sprout chia (a type of mint) from a terra-cotta figurine, first became popular in the United States in the 1980s. Some 500,000 of these "faux fur" companions are still sold annually.

OLIVER

BELLA

PET ON A PILLOW

CAT NAPPER

4 MOST POPULAR FIREHOUSE DOG

Though largely symbolic these days, Dalmatians' longtime association with firehouses is because of their fiercely protective nature. That disposition came in handy during the 1800s, when fire engines were pulled by horses. Horses and the equipment were a target for theft, so Dalmatians were used as watchdogs.

5 MOST POPULAR WAY TO SHOW YOUR PET SOME LOVE

What better way to prove to your pet that she's your favorite friend than to turn her likeness into a pillow! You can customize a pillow to look just like your dog, cat, or any other pet by sending in a photo to a company that will print it and even cut it out to the shape of your pet.

6 MOST POPULAR NAP BUDDY

An animal shelter in Wisconsin, U.S.A., doesn't mind if its volunteers sleep on the job. In fact, it encourages it! Retired schoolteacher Terry Lauerman, who visits the cage-free shelter almost every day, grooms the cats and then lies on the couch and naps with them for several hours. News of these catnaps went viral on the internet, bringing attention to the animal shelter, which rehabilitates cats with special needs.

DALMATIAN

DALMATIANS' POPULAR SPOTS

Dalmatians may be most famous for their signature black spots (they even have spots on the inside of their mouths!), but when they are born, Dalmatian puppies lack spots entirely. They are born pure white, and the spots begin to show up after a few weeks. And no two Dalmatians develop the exact same spot pattern. One description for a Dalmatian is a "plum-pudding dog," because the spots resemble the candied fruits and nuts found in the traditional British dessert of plum pudding.

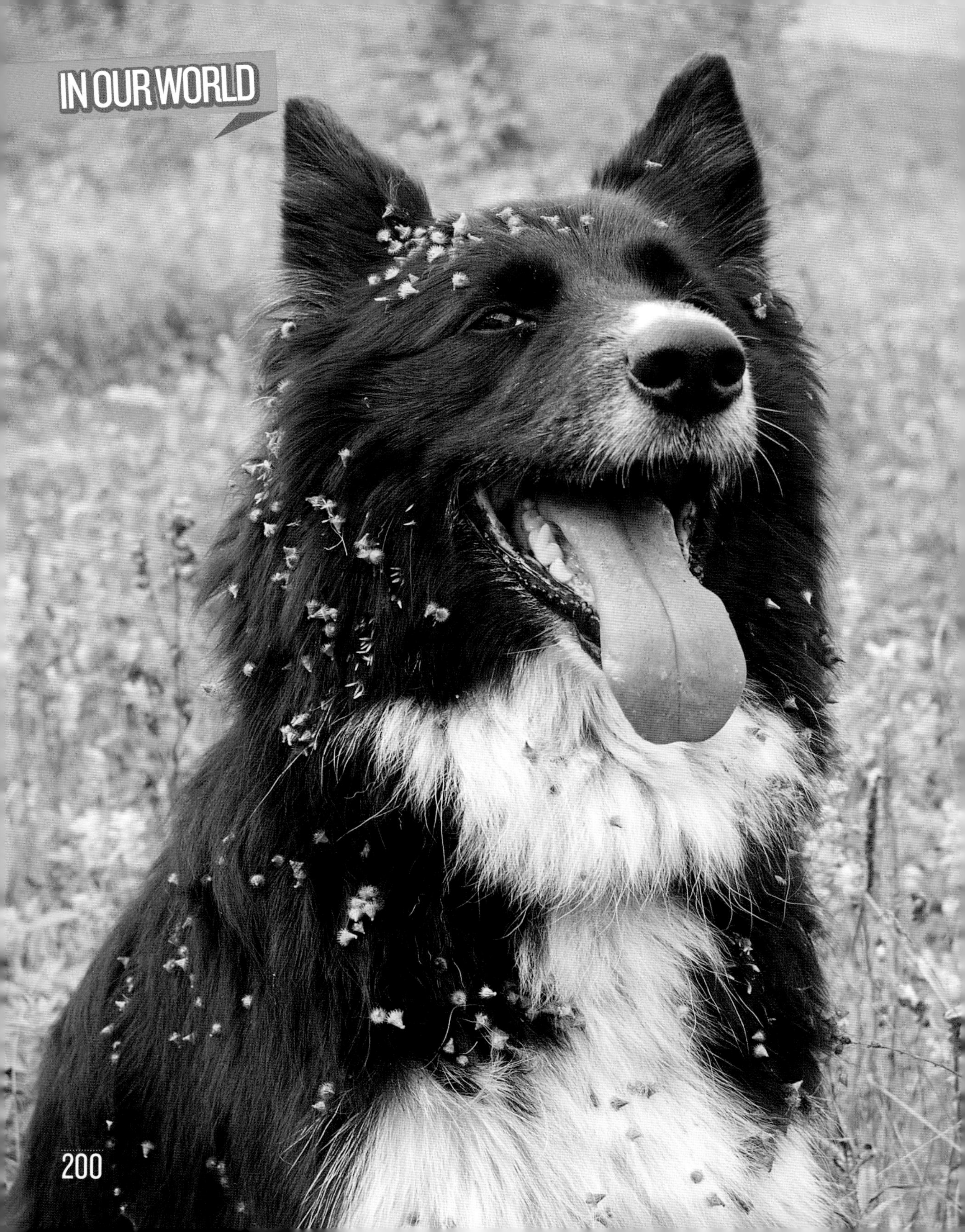

A BURR-FECT INVENTION!

A walk through the woods inspired one of the world's most popular products.

One day in 1941, the Swiss scientist Georges de Mestral went walking in the woods with his dog. When they got home, they were both covered in burrs—those sticky seed pods that can adhere to clothes with incredible strength. Because de Mestral was a scientist with a curious mind, he looked at the burrs under a microscope and began to puzzle out what made them so strong. He discovered that the burrs use a hook-and-loop system that causes them to adhere (stick) securely to one another. Sound familiar? De Mestral realized this could be replicated in everyday products, and in 1955, he formally patented Velcro.

Since Velcro hit the stores, people have found all kinds of uses for the fastener, from hiding a spare key to wrapping up computer cords to keeping clothes together. It's even been used to hold together two of the chambers in an artificial heart! The company that makes Velcro once estimated that the material would only start to lose its stick-to-itiveness after opening and closing it 50,000 times. No wonder NASA uses this tenacious wonder to make sure equipment and food packets don't float away as astronauts careen through space. You might use it for a more down-to-earth reason: to keep your shoes "tied."

"VELCRO" IS A COMBINATION OF THE FRENCH WORDS FOR VELVET AND HOOK.

BE A FRIEND TO PETS

You don't have to have a pet to be a fan of pets! If you don't have a pet at home right now—or maybe you have pets but would love to interact with different types of animals—there are lots of ways get some quality time with animal pals. Check out these suggestions, talk it over with your parents, and have fun getting to make some new furry, scaly, or feathery friends!

* Volunteer at an animal shelter or rescue organization.
* Become a pet sitter for your neighborhood!
* Have a neighbor who works long hours or has a hard time getting out to walk their dog? Offer to come over to play with their pup or take them out for exercise.
* Does your school have class pets? Ask the teacher if there are any duties you can help out with—like cleaning cages or filling water bottles and food bowls.
* Consider making your home a foster home for a pet! Many rescue organizations are looking for people who can care for kittens a few weeks before they are ready for adoption, or a dog who needs a home before its forever home is found.
* Look into helping out at your local barnyard or stable.
* Make some dog or cat treats for the pets in your neighborhood. (Be sure to ask pet owners before giving out treats).

Getty Images; 54 [UP LE], otsphoto/Shutterstock; 54 [UP RT], Ekaterina Kurakina/Dreamstime; 54 [LO LE], Liumangtiger/Dreamstime; 54 [LO RT], Premium Stock Photography GmbH/Alamy; 55 [UP LE], Giselle Azevedo/Getty Images; 55 [UP RT], AP/Shutterstock; 55 [CTR LE], Miroslav Hlavko/Dreamstime; 55 [CTR RT], Best dog photo/Shutterstock; 55 [LO LE], iweta0077/Shutterstock; 55 [LO RT], Isselee/Dreamstime; 56-5c, Juniors Bildarchiv/age fotostock; 59, Julius T. Csotonyi; 60 [UP LE], susafri/Getty Images; 60 [UP RT], Tomas1111/Dreamstime; 60 [LO RT], Juniors Bildarchiv/age fotostock; 61 [UP RT], Grossemy Vanessa/Alamy; 61 [LO LE], cynoclub/Shutterstock; 61 [LO RT], Eric Isselee/Shutterstock; 62-63, Ville Palonen/Alamy; 64 [UP LE], Stephanie Robey/Artville; 64 [UP RT], Iconotec; 64 [CTR LE], Dazb75/Dreamstime; 64 [CTR RT], Anat0ly/Getty Images; 64 [LO LE], Syda Productions/Shutterstock; 64 [LO CTR], Bokeh Art Photo/Shutterstock; 64 [LO RT], Iurii Kachkovskyi/Shutterstock; 65 [UP LE], cynoclub/Shutterstock; 65 [UP RT], Arco/Sunbird Images/age fotostock; 65 [CTR LE], st-design/Getty Images; 65 [CTR CTR], Chua Wee Boo/age fotostock; 65 [CTR RT], Oleg Kozlov/Shutterstock; 65 [LO LE], Lasse Ansaharju/Dreamstime; 65 [LO RT], jctabb/Getty Images

Chapter 3: 66-67, khmel/Getty Images; 68-69, mihtiander/Getty Images; 70, averess/Alamy; 71 [UP LE], Katharine Toft/Alamy; 71 [CTR], tsik/Getty Images; 71 [LO], Anobis/Getty Images; 72-73, Grigorita Ko/Shutterstock; 72 [LE], Byrdyak/Getty Images; 72 [RT] Robyn Fayers/School of Life Sciences University of Lincoln; 73, photovova/Shutterstock; 74-75, Sergey Fomin/Alamy; 75, Larry Williams & Associates/Getty Images; 76 [UP], Svetlana Pavlova/ITAR-TASS News Agency/Alamy; 76 [CTR], Bombaert Patrick/Alamy; 76 [LO], Thomas Temple/SWNS; 77 [UP], Caters News Agency; 77 [LO LE], Idenviktor/Dreamstime; 77 [LO RT], fotofrankyat/Getty Images; 78 [UP], Alex Milan Tracy/Sipa USA/Newscom; 78 [LO], Rommel Demano/Getty Images; 79, Alex Milan Tracy/Sipa USA/Newscom; 80-81, agustavop/Getty Images; 81, Rick Friedman/Corbis/Getty Images; 82 [UP LE], Ottoduplessis/Dreamstime; 82 [UP RT], Brian Arbuthnot/Dreamstime; 82 [LO LE], Lindsay Helms/Shutterstock; 82 [LO RT], Natalia Bachkova/Dreamstime; 83 [UP LE], Yiorgos GR/Shutterstock; 83 [UP RT], sgoodwin4813/Getty Images; 83 [CTR LE], Sergii Petruk/Dreamstime; 83 [CTR RT], Byrdyak/Getty Images; 83 [LO LE], Fasphotographic/Dreamstime; 83 [LO RT], mjf795/Getty Images; 84-85, Przemek Iciak/Shutterstock; 84 [UP LE], Apinan Tangsriwong/Dreamstime; 84 [UP CTR], Alexander Levchenko/Dreamstime; 84 [UP RT], Svetlana Serebryakova/Shutterstock; 84 [LO LE], aa3/shutterstock; 84 [LO CTR LE], Miroslav Hlavko/Dreamstime; 84 [LO CTR], kepong srichaichana/Shutterstock; 84 [LO RT], olgagorovenko/Getty Images; 85 [UP LE], waku/Shutterstock; 85 [UP CTR], Maygutyak/Getty Images; 85 [UP RT], Ulrich Mueller/Dreamstime; 85 [UP CTR], Viktar Malyshchyts/Shutterstock; 85 [LO CTR LE], Tim UR/Shutterstock; 85 [LO CTR RT], acceptphoto/Shutterstock; 85 [LO LE], Tim UR/Shutterstock; 85 [LO RT], Andreykuzmin/Dreamstime; 86, CBS Photo Archive/Getty Images; 87 [UP], Philippe Le Tellier/Getty Images; 87 [LO LE], Walt Disney Pictures/Entertainment Pictures/ZUMA Press/age fotostock; 87 [LO RT], A.F. Archive/Metro-Goldwyn-Mayer MGM/Alamy; 88 [UP LE], Barbara P. Fernandez/The New York Times/Redux; 88 [UP RT], Chronicle/Alamy; 88 [LO RT], Travfi/Shutterstock; 89 [UP], Andrew Michael/Alamy; 89 [LO LE], Sure Petcare; 89 [LO RT], Amy Kerkemeyer/Shutterstock; 90-91, Piotr Naskrecki/Minden Pictures; 92, Siegfried Kuttig - RF -2/Alamy; 93 [BACKGROUND], atalia Fedosova/Shutterstock; 93, alynst/Getty Images

Chapter 4: 94-95, imageBROKER/Alamy; 96-97, Dr Morley Read/Shutterstock; 98, Daniel Schoenen/imageBROKER/Alamy; 99 [UP], Yuryi Oleinikov/Shutterstock; 99 [CTR], Everita Pane/Shutterstock; 99 [LO], Haykirdi/Getty Images; 100-101, Zoonar GmbH/Alamy; 100 [UP], Geoffrey Arrowsmith/Alamy; 100 [LO], Greg Oakley/BIA/Minden Pictures; 101, Heidi and Hans-Juergen Koch/

Minden Pictures; 102-103, Waldemar Dabrowski/Shutterstock; 103, Juniors Bildarchiv/age fotostock; 104, Kristina Armstrong/EyeEm/Getty Images; 104 [LO], BeyondImages/Getty Images; 105 [UP], Alessandra Sarti/imageBROKER/Alamy; 105 [CTR], Rausch Zoltn/Getty Images; 105 [LO], Richard Peterson/Shutterstock; 106-107, Rodrigo Reyes Marin/AFLO/Nippon News/Alamy; 107, Kyodo News Stills/Getty Images; 108-109, Steve Simmons UK/Getty Images; 109, Ben Guthrie/Getty Images; 110 [UP], Tierfotoagentur/Alamy; 110 [UP RT], Sokratyks/Getty Images; 110 [LO LE], Luis Holzer/Dreamstime; 110 [LO RT], rojiman and umatan; 111 [UP LE], Tonkovic/Shutterstock; 111 [UP RT], LWA/Digital Vision/Getty Images; 111 [CTR LE], Yuri Kravchenko/Shutterstock; 111 [CTR RT], Gert Vrey/Shutterstock; 111 [LO LE], Bildagentur Zoonar GmbH/Shutterstock; 111 [LO RT], Rob kemp/Shutterstock; 112-113, Posh Puppy Boutique by Charles Lushear; 112 [UP], Jerry Glass and Larry Glass/Heartwood; 112 [LO], Annette Shaff/Shutterstock; 113 [UP], Sebastien Dufour/Gamma-Rapho/Getty Images; 113 [CTR], evernalla/Getty Images; 113 [LO], Go Pet USA; 114, DEA/A. Jemolo/Getty Images; 115, Werner Forman/Universal Images Group/Getty Images; 116 [UP LE], otsphoto/Shutterstock; 116 [UP RT], Jerry Redfern/LightRocket via Getty Images; 116 [CTR RT], Sunheyy/Dreamstime; 117 [UP LE], Puhhha/Dreamstime; 117 [LO LE], Windowsontheworldphotography/Dreamstime; 117 [LO RT], Juergen & Christine Sohns/Minden Pictures; 117 [UP LE], Fieryphoenix/Dreamstime; 118, Richard Sheppard/Alamy; 118 [LO], sarayut/Getty Images; 119 [UP], Peter Laurie/BIPs/Stringer/Getty Images; 119 [LO], Simon Browitt/Alamy; 120, graphicphoto/Getty Images; 121, RichLegg/Getty Images

Chapter 5: 122-123, luamduan/Getty Images; 124-125, Elles Rijsdijk/Alamy; 126, Jason Smalley/NPL/Minden Pictures; 127 [UP LE], Susan Feldberg/Alamy; 127 [CTR], Francis Apesteguy/Getty Images; 127 [LO], CathyKeifer/Getty Images; 128-129, Geoffrey Robinson/Alamy; 128 [LO], 24Novembers/Shutterstock; 129, Steve Heap/Shutterstock; 130, Mila Atkovska/Shutterstock; 131 [UP], DAJ/Getty Images; 132 [UP], Francesca Carsen; 132 [CTR], Craig Borrow/Newspix/Getty Images; 132 [LO], AP Photo/Erie Times-News, Greg Wohlford; 133 [UP], The Gisborne Herald; 133 [CTR], Grahm S. Jones, Columbus Zoo and Aquarium; 133 [LO], AP Photo; 134 [BACKGROUND], Vafiya/Shutterstock; 134, Washington Imaging/Alamy; 135, Brent Cizek; 136-137, praisaeng/Getty Images; 138 [UP LE], Ezzolo/Shutterstock; 138 [UP RT], MirasWonderland/Getty Images; 138 [LO LE & LO RT], NC1/Supplied by WENN.com/Newscom; 139 [UP LE], Squamish/Getty Images; 139 [UP RT], Lukas Blazek/Dreamstime; 139 [CTR], Panther Media GmbH/Alamy; 139 [LO], AdaCo/Shutterstock; 141 [BACKGROUND], Corbis Historical/Getty Images; 141, Science History Images/Photo Researchers/Alamy; 142 [UP LE], Myssi Rizzo/EyeEm/Getty Images; 142 [UP RT], Clarence Martin/Dreamstime; 142 [LO RT], Simon Shim/Shutterstock; 143 [UP LE], Ward Poppe/Shutterstock; 143 [LO LE], Chicken Hill Poultry, LLC; 143 [LO RT], Eric Lafforgue/Art In All Of Us/Corbis/Getty Images; 144-145 [BACKGROUND], Kurita Kaku/Getty Images; 144-145, Koichi Kamoshida/Getty Images; 146 [LE], Westend61/Getty Images; 146 [RT], GlobalP/Getty Images; 147 [UP], Hillary Kladke/Getty Images; 147 [CTR], Brooke Anderson Photography/Getty Images; 147 [LO], Grigorita Ko/Shutterstock

Chapter 6: 148-149, Caters News Agency; 151, Radek Mica/AFP/Getty Images; 152, Harald Toepfer/Shutterstock; 153 [UP], Michaela Schönfeldt/Dreamstime; 153 [CTR], Janina Kubik/Dreamstime; 153 [LO], Mark Lambert/Getty Images; 154-155, Jonathan Irish/National Geographic Image Collection; 154, hosphotos/Shutterstock; 155 [UP], Karel Zahradka/Shutterstock; 155 [LO], Douglas Sacha/Getty Images; 156, Akimasa Harada/Getty Images; 157, Claire Wilson/Getty Images; 158 [UP], Lisa Pinder; 158 [CTR], Barcroft/Getty Images; 158 [LO], Caters News Agency; 159 [UP], Callie Schenker; 159 [CTR], photokool/Getty Images;

159 [LO], Brian Cahn/Zuma Press/Alamy; 160-161, STR/AFP/Getty Images; 161 [LE], AP/Shutterstock; 161 [RT], Chris Hill/Shutterstock; 162-163, BlueOrange Studio/Shutterstock; 162, ZJAN/kamathesurfing//Newscom; 164 [UP LE], Bianca Grüneberg/Dreamstime; 164 [UP RT], tsik/Getty Images; 164 [LO LE], William Perry/Dreamstime; 164 [LO RT], EcoPrint/Shutterstock; 165 [UP LE], Makarova Viktoria/Shutterstock; 165 [UP RT], Hollysdogs/Shutterstock; 165 [CTR LE], Tierfotoagentur/S. Starick/Alamy; 165 [CTR RT], Wasitt Hemwarapornicha/Shutterstock; 165 [LO LE], Schanz, U./Juniors Bildarchiv GmbH/Alamy; 165 [LO RT], otsphoto/Shutterstock; 166-167, Jeff Schultz/Alaska Stock Images/age fotostock; 168-169, Nucleargalaxy/Dreamstime; 169 [CTR], Photo Researchers/Science History Images/Alamy; 170 [UP LE], Max_grpo/Shutterstock; 170 [UP RT], Shai Lighter; 170 [UP RT], Matt Jeppson/Shutterstock; 171 [UP LE], Bob and Pam Langrish KA9Photo/Alamy; 171 [LO LE], Judith Dzierzaw/Dreamstime; 171 [LO RT], Erik S Lesser/EPA-EFE/Shutterstock; 172-173, Lori Epstein/NGP; 174, Neil Lockhart/Shutterstock; 175 [UP], Fabian Kleinke/Shutterstock; 175 [LO], thka/Shutterstock

Chapter 7: 176-177, danz13/Shutterstock; 178-179, Ratnakorn Piyasirisorost/Getty Images; 180, Faba-Photography/Getty Images; 181 [UP], Imagevixen/RooM the Agency/Alamy; 181 [CTR], James Christensen/Minden Pictures; 181 [LO], Haveseen/Dreamstime; 182-183, Anatolich/Shutterstock; 182, Arterra/Universal Images Group via Getty Images; 183 [UP], Miroslava Kopecka/Dreamstime; 183 [LO], Grigorita Ko/Shutterstock; 184, Timothy A. Clary/AFP via Getty Images; 185 [UP], Mario Tama/Getty Images; 185 [CTR LE], Timothy A. Clary/AFP/Getty Images; 185 [CTR RT], Hector Acevedo/ZUMA Wire/Alamy; 185 [LO], Hector Acevedo/ZUMA Wire/Alamy; 186 [UP], Emma Lacey; 186 [LO], ullstein bild/Getty Images; 187 [UP], Sodeugra/Getty Images; 187 [CTR], Dee Dee Murry; 187 [LO], Tropical studio/Shutterstock; 188-189, Allison Whitfield-Smith; 189, Sprinkles Cupcakes, LLC; 190-191, Gerry Ellis/Minden Pictures; 191 [CTR], Gina Kelly/Alamy ; 192 [UP LE], Pipenko/Shutterstock; 192 [UP RT], WilleeCole Photography/Shutterstock; 192 [LO RT], Stewart Cook/Getty Images; 192 [LO LE], Jonathan Nguyen/le marcel dog bakery; 193 [UP LE], medveda/Shutterstock; 193 [UP RT], Smart-foto/Shutterstock; 193 [CTR LE], Ljupco Smokovski/Shutterstock; 193 [CTR RT], pyzata/Alamy; 193 [LO LE], Tim Gangloff/Cal Sport Media/Alamy; 193 [LO RT], Fred Kfoury II/Icon Sportswire/Getty Images; 194-195, Mylaphotography/Dreamstime; 194 [UP], Mirko Rosenau/Shutterstock; 194 [LO], Northsweden/Shutterstock; 195 [UP LE], LMPphoto/Shutterstock; 195 [UP RT], aaltair/Shutterstock; 195 [CTR], AustralianCamera/Shutterstock; 195 [LO LE], Aleksander Bedrin/Dreamstime; 195 [LO RT], Juliya Shangarey/Shutterstock; 196, FAY 2018/Alamy; 197, jurra8/Shutterstock; 198 [UP LE], Photo Melon/Shutterstock; 198 [LO LE], Mega Pixel/Shutterstock; 198 [LO RT], LynGianni/Getty Images; 198 [UP RT], Peter Dasilva/EPA/Shutterstock; 199 [UP LE], photosbyjim/Getty Images; 199 [UP RT], Wiskerke/Alamy; 199 [LO RT], Elizabeth Feldhausen; 200, Jackan/Shutterstock; 201, MBCheatham/Getty Images; 202, Soloviova Liudmyla/Shutterstock; 203 [UP], picturepartners/Shutterstock; 203 [LO], Oliver Wilde/Shutterstock; 204, Sergey Trifonov/Alamy; 205, Eatonphotography2019/Dreamstime; 206, BlazenImages/Getty Images; 207, mariakbell/Getty Images; 208, cookelma/Getty Images

CREDITS

Since 1888, the National Geographic Society has funded more than 12,000 research, exploration, and preservation projects around the world. The Society receives funds from National Geographic Partners, LLC, funded in part by your purchase. A portion of the proceeds from this book supports this vital work. To learn more, visit natgeo.com/info.

NATIONAL GEOGRAPHIC and Yellow Border Design are trademarks of the National Geographic Society, used under license.

For more information, visit nationalgeographic.com, call 1-877-873-6846, or write to the following address:

National Geographic Partners
1145 17th Street N.W.
Washington, DC 20036-4688 U.S.A.

Visit us online at nationalgeographic.com/books

For librarians and teachers: nationalgeographic.com/books/librarians-and-educators

More for kids from National Geographic: natgeokids.com

National Geographic Kids magazine inspires children to explore their world with fun yet educational articles on animals, science, nature, and more. Using fresh storytelling and amazing photography, *Nat Geo Kids* shows kids ages 6 to 14 the fascinating truth about the world—and why they should care. **kids.nationalgeographic.com/subscribe**

For rights or permissions inquiries, please contact National Geographic Books Subsidiary Rights: bookrights@natgeo.com

Designed by Nicole Lazarus

The publisher would like to acknowledge the following people for making this book possible: Kathryn Williams, associate editor; Jen Agresta, project editor; Julie Beer and Michelle Harris, authors; Sanjida Rashid, art director; Nicole Lazarus, designer; Lori Epstein, photo director; Shannon Hibberd and Alison O'Brien Muff, photo editors; Jennifer Geddes, fact-checker; and Anne LeongSon and Gus Tello, design production assistants.

Library of Congress Cataloging-in-Publication Data

Names: Beer, Julie, author. | Harris, Michelle, author.
Title: Pet records : the biggest, smallest, smartest, cutest, weirdest,
  and most popular pets on the planet/Julie Beer, Michelle Harris.
Description: Washington, DC : National Geographic Kids, 2020. | Includes
  index. | Audience: Ages 8-12 | Audience: Grades 4-6
Identifiers: LCCN 2019034686 | ISBN 9781426337352 (paperback) | ISBN
  9781426337369 (library binding)
Subjects: LCSH: Pets--Miscellanea--Juvenile literature.
Classification: LCC SF411.35 .B44 2020 | DDC 636.088/7--dc23
LC record available at https://lccn.loc.gov/2019034686

Printed in Hong Kong
20/PPHK/1